Skills and Techniques for Group Work with Children and Adolescents

Rosemarie Smead

Research Press
2612 North Mattis Avenue
Champaign, Illinois 61821

Copies of this book may be ordered from the publisher at the address given on the title page.

Composition by Tradewinds Imaging
Printed by Malloy Lithographing

ISBN 0–87822–352–5
Library of Congress Catalog Number 95–69455

*This book is fondly dedicated to the memory of
Frank Paul D'Angelo.
In our brief encounter you shared with me your gift
of determination and perseverance in adversity
and gently required that I rethink the value of family.
Thank you, Father Blue Eyes.*

CONTENTS

Section 2

Leadership Skills

Section 3

Therapeutic Interaction Techniques

FIGURES

ACKNOWLEDGMENTS

An abiding sense of love and gratitude fill my heart as I think of the hundreds of special persons who shared of themselves in my many workshops, classes, and training experiences over the years. It is their willingness to risk to learn, practice, and apply the essential group work skills and techniques, and to grow personally and professionally, that inspire me to record in this book the synthesis of my learning experiences.

As I travel around the country conducting training, I receive abundant "warm fuzzies" from counselors who are using my previous two books, *Skills for Living: Group Counseling Activities for Elementary Students* and *Skills for Living: Group Counseling Activities for Young Adolescents*, also published by Research Press. The children these counselors have reached are affirmed, validated, empowered, and loved because counselors care enough to learn the medium of group work to help them heal one another. I thank you and embrace you as we journey together, sharing our love for children and the miracles that happen in group with them.

Finally, my profound thanks to my dear friends at Research Press—Ann Wendel, Russ Pence, Karen Steiner, Dennis Wiziecki, and the rest of the family—for your scrupulous attention to detail, steadfast commitment to excellence, and support and encouragement through the process of bringing my three books to life.

INTRODUCTION

During my past two decades of teaching group work to counselors in training and conducting workshops and consulting across the country and internationally, I have realized that those of us who use the group work modality with children have few resources for learning and practicing skills and techniques specific to our endeavor. Group work is exciting, energizing, and reinforcing. It is also taxing, draining, and worrisome. Frequently, there is no one on site to help a counselor understand how to correct errors and improve practice, and so frustration can build. Many counselors have had only one course in group work some time ago, and perhaps all that remains from that is a grade on a faded transcript. It is impossible to cover the many complexities of group work process and dynamics, much less teach and practice a wide range of skills and techniques, in a course lasting only a quarter or semester.

My two previous books, *Skills for Living: Group Counseling Activities for Elementary Students* (Morganett, 1994) and *Skills for Living: Group Counseling Activities for Young Adolescents* (Morganett, 1990), present step-by-step plans for running groups on such topics as dealing with a family divorce, friendship skills, coping with grief and loss, peace-making skills, and others. The present volume augments these two books by describing the leadership skills and therapeutic interaction techniques you will need to be effective with young people in any type of group situation, whether open- or closed-ended, conducted in a school or other clinical setting. Each skill and technique includes a full description, rationale, suggestions for use, related resources, and specific suggestions for practice.

Section 1 focuses on critical professional issues and the organizational skills you will need to conduct successful groups with children and adolescents. The main topics covered are the nature of

1

group work, ethical guidelines and related professional issues, organizing the group experience, the group process, and ways to use problem situations as learning experiences. You will find suggestions here to begin, conduct, and evaluate the group experience.

Section 2 focuses on 14 group leadership skills. Leadership skills have been defined in a number of ways in the group literature. For example, Pearson (1981) divides leadership skills into the two areas of teaching skills and group management skills. Jacobs, Harvill, and Masson (1994) describe 12 different leadership skills. Corey and Corey (1992) describe 15 such skills. In brief, leadership skills are actions the leader purposefully takes to move the group toward its goals. These skills—for example, using activities and exercises, focusing, drawing out, and cutting off—pertain to the ongoing conduct of the group. Although in a real group setting these skills overlap, they are presented here separately to allow you to practice them one at a time. It will be best to read completely through this section, then select one skill to master. For example, you might decide to learn how to introduce and use activities and exercises. Or you might want to practice the skill of processing for several sessions until you have it well in hand. Then, as your comfort and confidence increase, you can combine skills. Before long you will notice that you are using a wide range of skills to maximize what is happening in group. Sometimes you will find that you have been using a particular skill but that you have used it without knowing why, or when it is most beneficial, or with whom to use it most effectively. By making the use of these skills a conscious matter, you can more easily select a skill on the spot, thus enhancing the experience for you and group members.

Section 3 describes 10 therapeutic interaction techniques— contracting, role-playing, "I" statements, and the like—by which therapeutic outcomes can be achieved. These more complicated, frequently theoretically based techniques are used to elicit a therapeutic action between or among members. The techniques can be used with the group as a whole or with individuals within the group as they work on their own issues, behavior change goals, and personal growth. Some of these techniques stand alone—that is, they can be used to bring about a therapeutic outcome by themselves. The self-as-model technique for helping children see themselves as successful in performing a goal behavior is an example of this type of technique. Others are "helper" techniques, to be used in conjunction with or as part of other learning or therapeutic experiences. Examples

2

of this type include role-playing and feedback. Mastering a range of therapeutic techniques will give you more ways to help children of different ages meet their group experience goals.

It is important to point out that, although some of the skills and techniques discussed in this book have been researched, the research generally relates to use with adult populations. Because group work with children is a recent phenomenon without an extended history of scientific study, most of these ideas have not been subjected to research scrutiny as they apply to this population. As presented here, the skills and techniques are based on my own years of experience with children in inpatient, outpatient, and academic settings. They reflect my own study of the literature and my own ways of dealing with issues that arise in facilitating group interaction. I have taught these skills to hundreds of counselors in training and inservice settings—through course work, internships, and experiential workshops—and they appear to affect both leadership and outcomes in a significant way.

I sincerely hope the ideas discussed here help you allow the children and adolescents you work with to be "stars," shining in the light of your guidance. I would welcome hearing about your experiences using these skills and techniques, and invite any suggestions for improvement. Best wishes, and peace and joy to you and your groups!

Resources

Corey, M. S., & Corey, G. (1992). *Groups: Process and practice* (4th ed.). Pacific Grove: Brooks/Cole.

Jacobs, E. E., Harvill, R. L., & Masson, R. L. (1994). *Group counseling: Strategies and skills* (2nd ed.). Pacific Grove, CA: Brooks/Cole.

Morganett, R. S. (1990). *Skills for living: Group counseling activities for young adolescents*. Champaign, IL: Research Press.

Morganett, R. S. (1994). *Skills for living: Group counseling activities for elementary students*. Champaign, IL: Research Press.

Pearson, R. E. (1981). Basic skills for leadership of counseling groups. *Counselor Education and Supervision, 21*(1), 30–37.

PROFESSIONAL ISSUES AND ORGANIZATIONAL SKILLS

Group counseling is not an event; it is a process that unfolds over time. As professional counselors who undertake group work with youths, we feel a special sense of responsibility toward our vulnerable clients and endeavor to provide an optimum experience for them in every way. We are aware of the powerful and healing effects of group participation and also of the potential for emotional pain. Because of our awareness and responsibility, we strive to learn and grow ourselves, both personally and professionally, so we can model and maximize the experience of becoming "real" for children.

Discussed in this section are the professional issues and organizational skills that form the foundation of the group work experience. The discussion of professional issues has implications for both group planning and our day-to-day conduct of groups. The organizational skills described clarify the steps in organizing, conducting, and evaluating your groups.

The Nature of Group Work

Types of Groups

A great deal of confusion exists about the types of groups offered to help people change and grow. Even within the educational and mental health professions the terms *support group, group therapy, group counseling,* and *group guidance* are unclear. The Association for Specialists in Group Work (ASGW), a division of the American Counseling Association, has described four major types of groups (ASGW, 1989): task/work groups, guidance/psychoeducation groups, counseling/interpersonal problem-solving groups, and psychotherapy/personality reconstruction groups. Figure 1 details the relationship

5

FIGURE 1

Types of Groups

Characteristics	Task/Work	Psychoeducation/Guidance	Counseling	Therapy
	Goal oriented	Preventive	Relationship	Relationship
	Accomplish task	Educational	Process	Process
	Implement decision making	Developmental	Problem oriented	Problem oriented
	Maintain attention on task/work issue	Cognitive	Affective	Affective
	Manage group conflict	Skill oriented	Behavior change	Behavior change
		Planned	Small group	Small group
		Large groups	Selected	Selected
		For all or self-selected	Confidential	Confidential
			3–6 months	Long-term personality change

Conducted by	Wide range of professionals Community committee	Teachers Nurses Counselors At-risk personnel Student assistance personnel Social workers Administrators	Licensed/certified mental health professionals with a minimum of a master's degree	Licensed/certified mental health professionals with a minimum of a master's degree and advanced group work training and supervision
Examples	Task force Learning group	Social skills training Career exploration AIDS education	Divorce issues Substance abuse Transition problems	Relationship issues Abnormal behaviors Unresolved loss/grief

among the types; it will be valuable as a handout or overhead when you explain proposed counseling efforts to teaching staff, administrators, or parents of potential group members. By understanding these distinctions, you will be able to help others understand what services you are actually providing for your client population.

Task/Work Groups

Task or work groups are defined as a broad range of groups where the application of group work principles facilitates the goals of the group. This type of group uses organizational and community group dynamics to work toward specific goals and includes, among others, learning groups, committees, study circles, task forces, and discussion or planning groups. Examples of this type would include a group of children who cooperate in designing and carrying out a science project or a group of adolescents who work together to raise money for the school band's annual trip.

Guidance/Psychoeducation Groups

Guidance groups are commonly found in a school setting, whereas psychoeducation groups are more frequently found in clinical, hospital, or other settings. This type of group uses group work dynamics and principles to bring about primary and secondary prevention of diagnosed or "at risk" populations. The leader in a guidance or psychoeducation group uses principles of human growth and development, developmental guidelines, environmental assessment, and the concept of empowerment to assist members.

Usually conducted in a large-group setting, this type of group provides members with information about specific problems and encourages them to make more effective decisions. Examples of this type include an educational group on the topic of AIDS and other sexually transmitted diseases for high school students or an ongoing guidance class in elementary school for learning friendship skills.

Counseling/Interpersonal Problem-Solving Groups

This type of group, usually called "group counseling," is significantly different from the two previously mentioned groups. Group counseling is process oriented, whereas task groups and guidance/psychoeducation groups are content oriented. In other words, counseling groups involve a process and a relationship between leader and group members. They exist to resolve usual but problematic issues developing in life that we need more specific and effective skills and competencies to handle. Some examples of educational, personal, career, and developmental topics served by group counseling include divorce, anger, uncomplicated grief and loss, relationship issues, friendship skills, and self-esteem. Often groups on such topics take place in schools and agencies that provide services to youths.

Psychotherapy/Personality Reconstruction Groups

A psychotherapy group focuses on the remediation of deep psychological problems and has as a goal major changes in personality and behavior. A group experience for adjudicated youths who engage in violent behaviors or a therapy group for children who have had traumatic life experiences (e.g., multiple deaths or history of extreme family instability) would fit this classification. This type of group is used in clinical settings rather than schools. Before conducting such a group, the leader must undergo extensive supervised educational experiences.

Content versus Process

Group classroom guidance and skills training are content oriented, whereas group counseling is process oriented. The intent and outcome of the two approaches are different. In group counseling, the purpose is to provide a safe environment for children to explore their feelings, values, attitudes, and ideas about themselves and their behavior, with behavioral and attitudinal changes as a result. The group members are encouraged to participate fully by making connections with one another and being supportive and encouraging of one another's situations and attempts to change behavior.

Content refers to what group members are talking about, the subject of the present conversation. If a group leader asks, "Today's topic is being assertive on dates. Who would like to share some ideas on the subject?" or conducts a go-around on what group members think about driving and drinking, that's content. Content is important as the basic raw material used to stimulate attitudinal and behavioral change among members. However, being content oriented keeps the group in the "there and then" rather than the "here and now." In other words, content is usually information, behavior, skills practice, and so forth that serve as a structure and give you the basic data to use as a springboard for developing ideas and relationships.

On the other hand, *process* refers to the nature of the relationship among the group members who are communicating with one another. Process-centered leadership focuses on the way individuals talk and what that means to the group experience. A process-centered leader requests group members to reflect and think about how they are interacting with one another as well as what is happening. In other words, process refers to relationships—what members are thinking, feeling, and doing right now in the group, not outside the session or in the past. Focusing on process, on the here-and-now, helps children learn to talk about immediate thoughts and feelings, which in turn may help them in their adult relationships.

Dealing with process and content equally is an essential group work leadership skill. By focusing on process, group members learn to express and hear feelings, give and receive feedback, and support one another in the here and now. But many group leaders favor content over process. One reason may be inadequate preparation at the master's level, resulting in lack of awareness of the importance of making here-and-now feelings, thoughts, and behaviors part of the group experience. Content is obvious and easier to deal with; the leader who is uncomfortable with or lacks knowledge in dealing with immediacy in relationships may avoid dealing with process because it is more confrontational and requires more advanced skills. In addition, some group leaders have been teachers for many years before becoming counselors, and, given their long history of being responsible for making sure content is learned, it may be difficult for them to change gears.

In the group, you must always be willing and ready to let go of the content of the session to deal with the immediacy of the relationships of group process. A basic guideline is to deal with events in the following order: what is presently happening in group, current events outside the group, and past events outside the group.

Leadership Style

Leadership style can be thought of as a continuum of control over the group. At one end of the continuum is leading, or complete control over the content and expectations of the session. This is similar to a classroom situation in which the teacher presents information in lecture style and each child interacts independently with the teacher and with the books and materials in front of him or her. Questions are also unilateral, between teacher and student, and little if any interaction takes place among the class members. The leader assesses the degree to which the children have assimilated the material presented.

10

On the other end of the continuum is the leadership style of facilitation. Facilitation involves shared responsibility for what happens in the session; the leader provides stimulus material, but the focus is on interpersonal actions, not on learning specific content. Generally, the group leader begins with a little more structure to provide the opportunity for security and trust to develop, then eases away from a structured leadership style to a more facilitative one, turning over the responsibility for change and growth and learning to the children in the group.

This approach may be new for someone accustomed to the content-oriented approach of the educational setting. But you will need to let go of some control for group counseling to succeed. You may need to give up the rigidity of an agenda for the needs of the moment. Many times in group work with children a member of the group will arrive obviously hurting over an incident or situation. It is essential that you acknowledge the child's immediate issue or emotional need rather than stay with the content. If the agenda is rigidly followed, the child with the issue will not be psychologically present in the group and the other children will likely wonder what is going on.

Young children are used to being in a more structured classroom setting than older children. Depending on their classroom experiences, their level of self-esteem, and other factors associated with personality and experience, they may be confused by the idea of sharing responsibility for what goes on in the group. They may have difficulty addressing their statements to another group member rather than to the leader, for example. Their hesitation can be overcome rather easily by the leader's establishing and reinforcing interaction among members. Children become accustomed to the new pattern of communication quickly and appear to enjoy the freedom to interact with one another and the leader on a different level.

In a time-limited, topic-driven group for children, it is probably best to function more at the leader end of the continuum early on in the group. This helps in establishing norms and getting the group started. As soon as group members are able, however, you will want to shift toward facilitation and encourage them to assume responsibility for working together.

Ethical Guidelines and Related Professional Issues

The cornerstone of every profession is its professional association's ethical guidelines for practitioners. Especially because we are

11

influencing the behavior of minors, as group counselors we must have a clear understanding of the ethical behavior expected of us. Those of us who practice group work can look to the ASGW's (1990) published ethical guidelines for help in practicing our specialty. These guidelines give support and clarification as we respond to the needs and responsibilities of group leadership. The complete guidelines are reproduced as Appendix A in this book. This section briefly discusses how these guidelines apply to group work with children and youths and examines some related professional issues.

Guideline 1: Orientation and Providing Information

An increased focus on consumer rights and responsibilities has amplified the issue of informed consent for medical and psychological treatment. Like adult group members, children need to know the purpose and goals of the group, what will or may happen in the group, and what the expectations are for leader and members. This information helps them make a choice regarding participation.

Because children are minors, the term *assent* is more accurate than *consent* because minors are not legally capable of giving consent. As group counselors, we need to ensure that every child accepted into the group experience has been given sufficient information about what will happen to give his or her assent to being a member. In the case of a legal minor, a parent (or parents) must give consent as well. Ways of obtaining consent are discussed in the following section on organizing the group experience.

The TAP-In Selection Checklist, presented as Appendix B in this book, enumerates what you need to tell and ask the child before selecting that child for a group. This extensive checklist covers most of the information that the guidelines indicate should be given to members before the group begins.

Children's developmental limitations make it more difficult to provide the necessary orientation and information for group participation, but as group leaders we must try as hard as we can to explain these issues in language children can understand.

Guideline 2: Screening of Members

It is particularly important to screen members in groups for children because children are especially vulnerable psychologically. Their level of cognitive development prevents them from thinking abstractly about potentially harmful aspects, such as the possibility of other children's being hurtful, the reemergence of negative feelings from a family tragedy such as a suicide, or the ramifications of someone in the group's breaking confidentiality. Affectively, children are usually poorly prepared to deal with intense feelings, especially if they occur suddenly and powerfully. Group work frequently involves the experience of intense feelings. Behaviorally, children have less well developed coping and social skills with which to deal with sudden insights, the aggressive responses of other children, and pressure to learn new behaviors. They are usually unable to understand why they are not a good candidate for a group and can take perceived rejection very hard. For all these reasons, I take the screening process more seriously than any other aspect of pregroup preparation.

Although a child might need therapeutic help desperately, group work might not be appropriate. Perhaps the child's issues are so severe as to draw more energy and time from the group than the particular group is able to provide. To have this child in the group could impede the group process or jeopardize the child's own well-being. If a particular member's needs are so great as to require more therapeutic energy, the other members of the group will not receive equitable treatment. It is much better to determine such matters before the group begins. Having the child start and then terminate the group is potentially painful to the child and disruptive to other group members.

Ultimately, it is the group leader who is ethically responsible for selecting group members to ensure the best possible outcome, and in the unfortunate event of litigation, the leader who could be held at fault for failing to screen out a child who might be in a fragile emotional state and negatively affected by the group experience. Because this is the case, the leader should be the one to determine who will belong to a particular group. Whether a certain member will be selected can also be a therapeutic team decision, as long as the group leader has the prerogative to accept or reject the child. More on screening and selecting children for group appears in the section on organizing the group experience.

Guideline 3: Confidentiality

Confidentiality is perhaps the most important issue in group work, both with children and adults, because without the assurance of confidentiality, group members will not develop sufficient trust to self-disclose. Self-disclosure is the "grist for the mill," and without it there is no group experience.

Although confidentiality is necessary to protect children's privacy so they feel safe self-disclosing, if a child's welfare or the welfare of others is compromised, you will be required to break confidentiality. A chart like the one shown in Figure 2, posted in your office and in the room where the group meets, can help everyone remember the limits of confidentiality. "Harm" refers to information about the child's having harmed or planning to harm himself or herself, another person, or physical property. "Abuse" refers to information about child abuse. "Courts" refers to a court's subpoena of counseling records or knowledge of a felony crime. In each of these cases you would be expected to divulge information to the appropriate authorities.

It is best to tell the children before the group even begins that confidentiality cannot be 100% guaranteed. Children of all ages seem to be able to deal with this concept if it is explained in an open and positive manner and in age-appropriate words. For specific ways to do this, see the leadership skill "Ground Rules and Other Norms."

Guideline 4: Voluntary/Involuntary Participation

Counseling is a voluntary effort to improve oneself. Change and personal growth cannot be legislated. Yet in some settings, such as inpatient treatment centers and juvenile court agencies, youths are required to participate in a group treatment experience. When you lead an involuntary group, you are ethically responsible for taking steps to ensure that the members are given the same information voluntary members receive about the group. Involuntary group members need to know that they have the same rights (and responsibilities) as voluntary members, except the right not to attend. Make every attempt to help involuntary members set goals, participate at their own level, and function in a manner similar to that of voluntary members.

Guideline 5: Leaving a Group

Except for those whose participation is involuntary, every member has the right to exit the group. Because leaving a group prematurely can negatively affect both the member who is leaving and the members left behind, you have the responsibility to assist this process in an appropriate way. The best way to do this is to explain before the group begins how terminations will be handled. Be sure each child understands that his or her exit has an impact on everyone

FIGURE **2**

Limits of Confidentiality

Harm
(to self or others)

Abuse

Courts

in the group and that if this is the child's choice, he or she will need to inform you before leaving. Sometimes having the child attend one final session to share this information and say good-bye to the other group members can help a child work through fears of dealing with problems and result in the child's remaining in the group. Even if the child does not decide to stay, this procedure supports the member's decision while at the same time respecting other group members' need to have closure on the situation.

Guideline 6: Coercion and Pressure

Coercion and pressure are part of any group. The ASGW guideline on this topic clarifies that it is important for the group leader to use appropriate therapeutic pressure to help group members focus on and deal with their issues and behavior problems. However, the group leader cannot exert "undue pressure" or permit other members to do so. In brief, it is your responsibility as the group leader to intervene when other members' attempts at persuasion become excessive. You must also protect against any physical or verbal aggression that might harm a member.

Physical aggression in a group of children might start out "friendly"—for example, tossing around a bean bag to indicate who has the floor might escalate to throwing the bean bag very hard at another group member. Such behaviors must be stopped as soon as they are recognized and the anger discussed directly. If anger is expressed verbally, you can use this as an opportunity to teach group members how to express their anger appropriately rather than shouting, name-calling, or using other aggressive tactics. Because a group is a natural forum for emotions, it is best to monitor the situation closely and avoid situations that have a high potential for someone's getting hurt.

Guideline 7: Imposing Counselor Values

As adults, it is our responsibility to teach children certain values, and yet there is great controversy regarding which values should be imparted to children in the school or mental health setting. Sometimes as adults we try too hard to push certain values. For example, we might stress the appropriateness of assertion without considering the possibility that a child from another culture might have been taught that being assertive is disrespectful and unacceptable for children. Or we might emphasize using direct eye contact without realizing that some

Asian and Hispanic/Latino cultures regard such behavior as rude and disrespectful.

In group work with children, you must help identify and respect individual differences concerning culture, race, religion, life-style, age, disability, gender, or values. Much is being written in the counseling journals and newer textbooks about the need to take into account the specific differences in the values and behaviors of the children with whom we work. It is our responsibility to keep up with this information and apply it in our practice. Sensitivity to the values of children's families of origins and a working knowledge and skill base are essential.

Guideline 8: Equitable Treatment

Equitable treatment means that we must try continually to be aware of favoritism as well as to ensure that each child's opinions, needs, and values are heard. It is natural to find some children more appealing than others, but is unethical to show bias toward or against a particular child, and favoritism or exclusion must be guarded against. Another aspect of equitable treatment concerns the responsibility to allow each child approximately equal time in the group to meet his or her needs. You will need to monitor the time closely so high self-disclosers or monopolizers don't take the time that shyer, lower self-disclosing children need.

Guideline 9: Dual Relationships

A dual relationship exists when counselor and group member have some other connection than as counselor and client, as would be the case, for example, if the group leader were also the teacher, nurse, or relative of a child in the group. Dual relationships result in an unfair balance of power and can lead to impaired judgment on the part of the counselor and a compromised ability to participate on the part of the group member.

Each child needs to be able to develop a trusting therapeutic relationship so that self-disclosure occurs, and this is not possible if the child also must experience the group leader in another role. It is difficult enough for us as adults to keep our many roles from contaminating one another at times, and it is impossible to expect a child to keep them separate.

Dual relationships can also exist between group members, with similar detrimental effects on group participation. For example,

17

siblings or relatives are more likely to engage in behaviors to maintain their family image rather than participate fully and should not be allowed in the same group because of this dual relationship.

Guideline 10: Use of Techniques

Ethical issues may arise over the use of counseling techniques. Before using a technique, you should be able to describe its theoretical underpinnings and the rationale for its use. Only those techniques or interventions that you have been trained and/or received supervision in should be used. You should also have had training commensurate with the impact of the technique on the child. For example, if you want to use a technique that has the potential to evoke strong emotions, you must know exactly what to do when a child reacts strongly, how to handle the reactions of other children in the group, and how to turn this into a learning experience. Otherwise, it is best to avoid the use of activities or exercises that evoke high affect until you have received further training.

Mastery of a technique with adults does not necessarily ensure its success with children and adolescents. For example, the gestalt "empty chair" technique is often used in grief work to help the client say good-bye to a loved one. This technique may not be appropriate for children: Although the experience may be positive for fairly mature adolescents, younger children may simply not understand the idea of talking to someone who isn't there, and older children may become overly emotional when this powerful technique is used.

Guideline 11: Goal Development

Many children do not know how to develop goals, whether they are short, medium, or long term. It is your responsibility as group leader to help them learn to develop realistic personal goals and to work toward them.

This guideline also concerns the importance of your developing goals for the group. If your goals are unclear, participation during the session and compliance with out-of-session activities or practice will be low.

Guideline 12: Consultation

In group counseling experiences, situations occur in which a member needs to be seen between sessions. Sometimes the request to be seen comes directly from the child. As the group leader, you must set and state a policy about between-session consultations. With such a policy in place, members will be less likely to use between-session consultations as a way of avoiding dealing with issues that belong in the group. For example, suppose a particular child acts out during group. If you see that child between sessions to rehash group rules and expectations, you rob the group of the opportunity to deal with the situation. Keeping the situation in the group allows the group process to unfold, gives group members the opportunity to share how they feel about the acting-out child's behavior, and allows the child to receive important feedback about how his or her behavior affects others.

Guideline 13: Termination from the Group

This guideline reminds us to monitor group members' progress closely and help promote termination from the group experience in a timely manner. Groups for children tend to be time-limited, and it is more likely that a group will end too soon than that members will stay beyond the group's usefulness to them. With this population, a more central issue is the way termination is handled. In a time-limited group, the group members know at the beginning that there will be a certain number of sessions, whereas in open-ended groups members leave when they have dealt with their issues. In either case, you will need to make the members aware of the upcoming end of their group experience and help them develop plans to evaluate their progress and follow up afterward. The ending of group or a child's leaving group presents the opportunity to teach children healthy ways of letting go of relationships and saying good-bye. (See the discussion of "Closing Rituals" in Section 3 for more on this subject.)

Guideline 14: Evaluation and Follow-Up

During a group experience, children's awareness of thoughts, feelings, and behaviors related to the topic is usually heightened. Plans are made to practice new behaviors, and support is available for everyone. After the group ends, that support and safety net are no longer there. It is important to plan some type of follow-up meeting, perhaps 3 to 4 weeks after the last session, to check in on group members' progress and support needs. In this way some closure can be brought to the experience and referrals made for children who need further help.

Guideline 15: Referrals

Sometimes after a child is selected for and begins a group, unexpected problems arise. If so, that child will need to be referred to more appropriate services. For example, if a youth unexpectedly reveals that he has been giving serious thought to suicide, you would need to see him individually to assess the risk potential, inform the parents, and make a referral to a therapist to work on the source of the issues. If a teenage girl reveals that she is "probably pregnant," you would need to work with her to share this information with her parents, receive immediate medical attention, and perhaps refer her to a mental health counselor who specializes in working with pregnant teens.

Guideline 16: Professional Development

It is unethical for counselors to use techniques or approaches beyond their level of training and supervision. For example, attending a hypnosis seminar for a weekend does not impart sufficient knowledge and skills for transfer to a group experience.

Group work is one of the most complicated of all counseling modalities, and we need to be aware of our own level of competence. We have an obligation to continue learning and growing. In order to stay current with the information in our specialty we need to belong to professional associations, participate in continuing education, and build a network of mental health and other professionals to give us support. Without effort invested in acquiring new knowledge, skills, techniques, and resources we will quickly fall behind in our ability to provide counseling and related services to our young clients.

One of the best ways to keep up to date is by reading the professional journals and newsletters available through membership in ASGW (5999 Stevenson Avenue, Alexandria, Virginia 22304). Through such materials you can keep abreast of practice ideas and continuing education and training on new developments as applied to groups. Group work is an exciting field, and the people who practice it are usually willing to share their ideas, techniques, and encouragement.

As counseling professionals we must consider, in addition to specific ethical issues, certain matters that affect our philosophy, practice, and interaction with colleagues on a regular basis. These professional issues are briefly highlighted here as they relate to the practice of group work with youths.

Psychological Risk

Children are especially vulnerable to psychological harm. Even though you explain the possibility of hurtful things occurring, the child's lack of life experience and cognitive development may make it difficult for you to feel comfortable that the child truly understands this information. It is critical for you to take every step possible to protect youngsters against the risks of psychological harm, whether intentional or unintentional.

Specific risks in groups with children include the chance of hostile confrontations by other group members, the risk that other group members might not keep disclosures confidential, the chance of experiencing or reexperiencing psychological pain, and so forth.

Commitment to the Value of Freedom

In terms of group work with youths, a commitment to freedom means that we encourage children to look at all possible options available in life situations, help them learn to weigh these options according to what is best for themselves and their families, and make intelligent choices based on this knowledge. It is important for us to value the freedom of each child to behave and believe as he or she chooses, insofar as it is not unlawful or harmful to others.

Willingness to Model

As counselors we value being authentic, honest, caring, supportive, competent, and genuine. If these and other values are important to us, then it is important that we be willing to model these behaviors for children. Youngsters are very quick to pick up on phony behaviors, and they invariably tune out adults who say one thing and do another.

Modeling also refers to our willingness to practice a skill or activity in the group session. For example, if you ask for a go-around on how members are feeling about group that day, be ready to be the first one to say how you are feeling so members understand what is expected and get some insight into your own emotions.

Developing Tolerance for Ambiguity and Frustration

A high tolerance for ambiguity and frustration is a virtue highly prized in our specialty. With so many interpersonal interactions going on at once, the frustration can be overwhelming at times! As group leader, you must allow members to learn and grow at their own pace.

Sometimes you may feel as though the group is going nowhere because there doesn't seem to be much progress at the beginning. Keep on setting the norms, encouraging, reinforcing, modeling, and developing your tolerance for not knowing or being able to control everything. Things will come along!

Pursuing Your Own Counseling

All of us go through rough spots and at times find ourselves perplexed by overwhelming experiences in our personal lives. At these times our judgment becomes clouded and our ability to provide support and skillful, competent counseling is interrupted. It is important that we be willing to seek our own counseling and help ourselves heal; otherwise we are impaired in our functioning and unable to be emotionally and physically present for our young clients.

Organizing the Group Experience

The group experience involves a sequence of interrelated events that fall generally into three categories.

Pregroup responsibilities

1. Conducting a needs assessment

2. Developing a written proposal

3. Advertising the group

4. Developing an accountability strategy

5. Accomplishing the selection process

6. Preparing resources

Active group events

7. Conducting the sessions

Postgroup responsibilities

8. Administering the posttest

9. Completing the evaluation procedure

10. Conducting the postgroup follow-up session

The following discussion will give you a sense of what needs to occur and approximately when it needs to occur during the process of conducting a group. Some of the comments reflect the reality that most groups for children and adolescents are both time limited and topic driven. The steps described are not set in stone; some might be better in a slightly different order for your setting, and sometimes several steps will be going on at once. Although the sequence might suggest it, there really isn't an "end" to the group experience. Because the group encourages new attitudes and behaviors, the personal transformations continue even after the sessions are over.

Step 1: Conducting a Needs Assessment

You probably serve more than one constituency in your setting. For example, if you are in a school, your constituents are the children, their parents, the teachers, the administrators, and, potentially, persons in the community. If you are in a service agency, your constituents might be youths, their parents, and possibly other persons working in the agency. By requesting feedback from the target population through needs assessments given periodically, you can determine what types of groups need to be offered. These groups may be developmental, topic oriented, or problem specific.

A needs assessment is important to stay fully informed about the current needs of your constituents. Without tapping in to them on a regular basis, you may be providing services that are not relevant or that do not accurately meet their requirements. Not only does a needs assessment tell you what topics are important, it provides you with data useful in persuading reluctant administrators and teachers to permit children to leave the classroom for the group experience.

There are formal and informal ways to conduct a needs assessment. In a school setting, you could informally poll parents, teachers, children, and administrators by directly asking them for their opinions on what group topics/issues need to be addressed. A more formal way to gather this important data is to develop a simple survey instrument that can more accurately assess the current state of needs, thus providing more in-depth information for both planning and evaluating future groups. Figure 3 provides an example of such an instrument.

In addition to specific topical groups, you may want to consider the need for more general, non-topic-driven group experiences. If you provide such groups, you will be able to meet needs that might

FIGURE **3** _____

Sample Group Counseling
Needs Assessment for Faculty

Dear Teacher:

Your school counselor will be conducting time-limited topical group counseling activities for children this year. We would like to have your input so that we can better meet your needs and the needs of the children in our school. Please be a part of helping us provide the best services possible so that our children have the opportunity to meet their full potential. Each of the following represents a major topical issue to be covered by an eight-session group counseling experience, with approximately eight children in a group. Each group will be led by a counselor or counselor team. Please help us determine which topics you think need to be covered by placing a check mark beside the topic. Put two check marks beside each of your top two priorities. Add any other topics you think need to be addressed. Thank you very much!

_____ 1. Learning peacemaking skills

_____ 2. Feeling better about yourself (self-esteem)

_____ 3. Learning how to make and keep friends

_____ 4. Dealing with a divorce in your family

_____ 5. Dealing with the death of a person or pet

_____ 6. Learning better ways of dealing with angry feelings

_____ 7. Learning to take responsibility for yourself at home and school

_____ 8. Understanding social responsibilities and values as part of a group (good citizenship)

_____ 9. Other _____

_____ 10. Other _____

Name _____ Date _____

Return to _____

not be covered by the more specific topics. Such a group might be called the "Growing-up Club" at the elementary level or "Life Skills" for older youths.

Step 2: Developing a Written Proposal

A proposal is a document with a specific purpose. First, it helps you organize what you are going to focus on in the group, describing the goals, objectives, and content of the group. Second, it serves as an aid to answer questions about the nature of the group to administrators, parents, teachers, colleagues, referral agencies, or funding sources. Perhaps you are in an elementary school setting where group counseling has never been a part of the counseling services. If so, there will be many questions from both colleagues and parents about what group counseling is all about. You will need to have done your homework in advance by having a solid proposal to demonstrate that you have a clear understanding of what will occur. The proposal will also demonstrate to an astute administrator that you are a knowledgeable professional who is competent in this area and understands the process from a variety of perspectives.

The written proposal should include the following types of information. These guidelines are based generally on recommendations provided by Corey and Corey (1992) in *Groups: Process and Practice*.

Description and Rationale

Describe the group as a time-limited group experience to learn new skills, practice more adaptive behaviors, and share ideas, thoughts, feelings, and interests on specific topics.

What is your purpose in conducting the group?

Whose needs does it meet?

What topics will be explored?

Objectives

What objectives do you have in mind for the group?

Are the objectives reasonable for the age and abilities of the participants?

Are the objectives clear? Measurable? Reasonable for the length of the group?

Logistics

Who will lead the group?

What are the leader's qualifications?

Who will be responsible for making sure ethical guidelines are followed?

How will group members be selected?

When will the group meet? If during school time, do all parties (parents, teachers, students) agree?

How many members will be selected, and what are the inclusion criteria?

Is there a plan to provide services for those who are not selected?

Where will the group meet, and for how long?

Will the group be closed or open to new members as it progresses?

How will the situation be handled if a member wants to drop out?

Procedures

What kinds of techniques will you be using?

How and when will you explain the risks involved in being a group member?

How will you protect members from being hurt physically or psychologically?

Will you take special precautions because participants are legal minors?

How will you explain confidentiality and its limits?

How will you handle requests from parents or others who might want you to divulge a child's confidences from group?

How will you obtain informed consent from the parent or guardian and informed assent from the child?

Will you require both parents to sign an informed consent if there is a noncustodial parent?

Are you using any recording devices or conducting any research?

How will you ensure safety and confidentiality of counseling records?

Evaluation

How do you plan to determine whether a member has changed due to the group experience?

How are you going to determine whether your goals and objectives have been met?

What follow-up procedures do you anticipate?

Who will receive evaluation data about the group?

How will evaluation data be stored?

Who will have access?

How do you plan to evaluate leader performance?

You can also include specific outlines of the sessions for some of the group topics you plan to cover. Figure 4 shows a sample session outline from *Skills for Living: Group Counseling Activities for Elementary Students* (Morganett, 1994). Many other session outlines for topical groups appear in this source, as well as in the other volume in the series (Morganett, 1990).

Step 3: Advertising the Group

After you have received approval for the group counseling experience, you will want to let your administrators and colleagues know what is happening. In both school and agency settings, these individuals will often be in a position to refer potential group members.

You are in the best position to determine how to advertise the group counseling experience in your setting. Use whatever media are available, including newsletters to teachers or parents, bulletin board announcements, notices and information centers, other colleagues in practice with youth, and so on.

If you have included colleagues, administrators, and teachers in the needs assessment, they will already know what is happening and will be able to keep an eye out for referrals. The children will refer themselves when they hear what is happening, and usually

FIGURE **4**

Sample Session Outline: Friendship Zingers

Goals

1. To increase awareness of what kinds of behaviors are damaging to friendships

2. To help children understand how other people perceive their friendship behaviors

3. To encourage children to use brainstorming as a technique to discover alternative ways to deal with friendship situations

4. To help children reinforce one another for modeling and sharing positive behaviors

Materials

A healthy snack, such as raisins in individual boxes, fruit, crackers, or juice (optional)

Group Session

Review

1. Welcome the children to group. Briefly go over the ground rules and the confidentiality rule.

2. Ask the children if they have anything they want to share about the last session, on the benefits of having older friends, animal friends, and imaginary friends.

3. Ask whether group members had the opportunity to introduce themselves to a new friend since the last session, and, if so, what this experience was like.

Working Time

1. Discuss the fact that friendships are very precious to us and that they add a great deal to our lives: We have friends all through our lives, and no matter where we live or move, we can keep old friends we love and make new friends. But if we don't treat a friend right or if we behave in a hurtful or embarrassing way,

someone might stop being friends with us, just as we might stop being friends with someone if that person treated us badly. Sometimes we make good choices in friendship behavior, and sometimes we make bad choices.

2. Explain that bad friendship choices are "friendship zingers," then ask the children to listen to the following situations as you read them. After you read each situation, ask, "What is the bad choice of behavior (the zinger)? What would be a better choice?"

Situation 1: Keshia is nosy. She walks up to kids who are talking and listens in on what they are saying. Then she goes and tells other kids what they were saying. No one likes her. Everybody calls her "nibby nose."

Situation 2: Kareem is a tattletale. Every chance he gets he runs and tells the teacher, his mom, or some other adult about the behavior of one of the other kids. The kids hate this, and no one will ask Kareem to play.

Situation 3: Paul is rude. He makes cutting remarks about everybody to make a joke. He says nasty things and makes fun of people, and then he can't understand why no one wants to have him for a friend. The more the kids dislike him, the more he is rude and tells them to bug off and get lost.

Situation 4: Karen uses foul language. She thinks it is cute and "grown up," and she puts down other kids who don't want to sound so rough and nasty. She is not aware that it makes her sound foolish and immature or that other kids don't want to be around her.

Situation 5: Lee is always dirty. He does not take a bath for days and days, and he comes to school smelling awful. His fingernails are a mess, and his hair is greasy, smelly, and never combed. His mother is always after him, but he refuses to take care of himself. The other kids don't even like to be around him.

Figure 4 (continued)

Situation 6: Phil does several unpleasant and annoying things. He picks his nose, spits on the sidewalk, and scratches himself in public. It is embarrassing to be his friend because he does these things, so no one wants to be around him. He thinks he is cool, that the other kids are babies and jerks, and that his behavior is OK.

3. If you have time, encourage children to role-play the situations and change the bad choice of behavior to a good choice. Try at least two or three so they can see the good choice of behavior being modeled.

Process Time

1. Discuss the following questions:

What did you learn today about things that can turn kids off to you as a friend?

How would you feel if you heard that you were doing some of these things that turn kids off?

What was it like for you to hear about other kids' problems with friendship?

What kind of courage does it take to tell your friend that he or she is doing something that turns you off?

Are you willing to try to change some of the things you might be doing that bother other kids so that you can have friends?

What could you or would you practice before we meet the next time?

2. Share snacks, if desired. Before saying good-bye, thank the children for coming to group and remind them of the meeting time for the next session.

you will have many more children who want and need to be in the group than space will allow.

Step 4: Developing an Accountability Strategy

Accountability has emerged as a crucial factor in funding decisions made about school and mental health services. A series of events have contributed to this trend, including the National Defense Education Act in 1958, the Community Mental Health Centers Act in 1963, and the *A Nation at Risk* report of 1983 (Gardner, 1983). Increasingly, we have come under pressure to demonstrate exactly what mental health counseling is and how well we do it.

As a profession, we are acutely aware of the complex interrelationships among personal relationships and emotions. The difficulty of our work sometimes even contributes in part to the perception that it is not possible or advisable to measure personal growth or counseling effectiveness. Also contributing to the problem is a general lack of preparation that would equip mental health personnel at the master's level to conduct evaluations. Nonetheless, by evaluating group work we are able to obtain feedback on what we need to improve on professionally and demonstrate the need for continued services. By avoiding evaluation, we foster lack of support from program and school administrators and permit the value of our work to be questioned and misunderstood.

Group work takes a great deal of time and energy, and everyone is interested in ascertaining whether the time and expertise of personnel are worth the investment—in other words, whether the group has met its goals. Figure 5 shows some typical client needs and group goals for this population.

An evaluation of the group's outcomes is central to accountability. Commercially produced tests or assessment instruments (anger assessment scales, self-esteem inventories) do exist for some of the topics and problems that you might be dealing with in a group for children. If a high level of validity and reliability is required, standardized tests are best. There are many other ways to evaluate group outcomes—some very complex. The work of Gazda (1989), Bruckner and Thompson (1987), Ehly and Dustin (1991), and Stone and Bradley (1994) will be of interest if you want to pursue further study in this area. You can also use a nearby college or university as a source for consulting help in research and evaluation.

FIGURE **5**

Client Needs and Group Goals

Client Needs	Group Goals
Deal with family divorce	Learn coping skills and share feelings and experiences; develop a support network
Improve study and school survival skills	Learn and practice better ways to get along with others and make better grades
Meet and make new friends	Learn prosocial skills that will transfer to daily activities
Reduce fighting and aggression	Learn alternative and more positive ways to express anger

If the information is going to be used to give general feedback to the children, parents, or other concerned adults, complicated assessment measures and statistics are probably unnecessary. Brief group experiences (8 to 14 sessions) are unlikely to produce statistically significant behavior change. However, a simple counselor-constructed Likert-type scale like the one shown in Figure 6 can help you assess attitudinal or belief changes resulting from the group experience.

Such scales are specifically geared to the issues, skills, and problems of a particular group—in this case, the topic of family divorce. Note that all of the items on this example are phrased so that a higher number (e.g., a 4 or 5) suggests a more desirable response and a lower number (e.g., a 1 or 2) suggests a less desirable response. More sophisticated evaluation measures are constructed so desirable responses are indicated by either high or low values; doing so decreases the chance that respondents will guess that a higher (or lower) number always indicates a desirable response, thus increasing the measure's reliability. Constructing the items so desirable responses are indicated by only one end of the scale may decrease the scale's reliability; however, it greatly simplifies data analysis. Again, if

FIGURE **6** _____

Sample Likert-Type Scale:
Dealing with a Divorce in the Family

Instructions: Each of the statements below concerns your ideas, beliefs, attitudes, or feelings about divorce. After each statement is a response you could choose. Circle the response that is how you think or feel now.

Scale

    1 = never

    2 = hardly ever

    3 = sometimes

    4 = most of the time

    5 = always

1. Divorce is better than having your mom and dad fight all the time.   1   2   3   4   5

2. I know I can talk about my new stepfamily members to others.   1   2   3   4   5

3. I have a support system of friends who understand me.   1   2   3   4   5

4. I like having stepbrothers and/or stepsisters.   1   2   3   4   5

5. I can express my feelings about the divorce.   1   2   3   4   5

6. I can talk with my parents about the divorce, and they will listen to me.   1   2   3   4   5

7. I know how to get along with stepbrothers and/or stepsisters.   1   2   3   4   5

8. I can deal with changes in visiting arrangements.   1   2   3   4   5

Figure 6 (continued)

9. It's OK for parents to get remarried   1   2   3   4   5
   after they divorce.

10. Talking about divorce with other   1   2   3   4   5
    kids who have the same problems
    helps me feel better.

---

reliability is critical to your evaluation, it would be best to use standardized measures.

When such a counselor-constructed scale is given as a pretest and posttest, the data collected can be used in two ways: (a) to help an individual child understand and work on his or her particular issues and (b) to give an overall idea of how the group appears to have changed in attitudes and beliefs. In either case, you would give the instrument as a pretest before the first session of the group, give the same instrument as a posttest a week or two after the last session of the group, then compare the pretest and posttest scores.

Data Analysis for an Individual Group Member

Figure 7 shows how the pretest and posttest scores can give you information about attitudinal change in an individual group member, Shawn. To construct a similar chart, take the following steps:

1. Enter the numerical value for each pretest item in the "Pretest Score" column.

2. Enter the numerical value for each posttest item in the "Posttest Score" column.

3. Subtract the posttest scores from the pretest scores for each item, then enter that number in the "Difference" column.

In looking at pretest/posttest scores for a single group member, you are concerned that the direction of change be in the hoped for or expected direction. As shown in Figure 7, Shawn answered Item 1 ("Divorce is better than having your mom and dad fight all the time") "hardly ever" (a score of 2) on the pretest, and "most of the time" (a score of 4) on the posttest. Because one would hope that a child would realize that divorce can at least provide an end to continual anger and fighting, Shawn's response suggests that his attitudes have changed in the hoped-for direction. However, his response on Item 8 ("I can deal with changes in visiting arrangements") is not in the expected direction. Shawn's pretest response was "most of the time" (a score of 4). His posttest response, "hardly ever" (a score of 2), suggests a regression in attitude, possibly reflecting his reassessment of his own coping skills. Such a response also could be the result of a recent negative real-life experience that is overpowering an attitudinal change.

What you could say by comparing pretest scores with posttest scores for each item is that Shawn appears to have had either no changes or positive changes in attitudes and/or beliefs on Items 1, 2, 3, 4, 5, 6, 9, and 10, or 80% of his responses. Twenty percent of his responses (Items 7 and 8) appear to show a regression. Alternatively, you could separate out the no-change items from the positive direction items and indicate that there were 60% positive responses, 20% neutral or no-change responses, and 20% negative responses.

FIGURE **7**_____

Data Analysis for an Individual Group Member

Item Number	Pretest Score	Posttest Score	Difference
1	2	4	+2
2	2	4	+2
3	1	4	+3
4	3	3	0
5	3	3	0
6	2	5	+3
7	3	2	-1
8	4	2	-2
9	1	3	+2
10	1	3	+2

Data Analysis for All Group Members

In order to evaluate attitudinal change in all group members, you figure a mean score for all members on each item, then determine the direction of change for each item. Figure 8 shows this type of data analysis for the whole group. To construct a similar chart, take the following steps:

1. Begin with the pretests. First list each group member's numerical response for Item 1. To derive the mean response for this item, add these numbers, then divide the sum by the number of children in the group (see the example in Figure 9).

2. Repeat this procedure to derive a mean score for each of the other pretest items. Enter all of these means in the "Pretest Score (Mean)" column.

3. Calculate the means for each posttest item in the same way, then enter them in the "Posttest Score (Mean)" column.

4. Subtract the pretest means from the posttest means and enter these numbers in the "Difference" column. This number indicates the amount of change from pretest to posttest.

FIGURE **8** _____

Data Analysis for All Group Members

Item Number	Pretest Score (Mean)	Posttest Score (Mean)	Difference
1	2.9	4.7	+1.8
2	1.9	4.3	+2.4
3	3.0	2.1	-0.9
4	1.8	3.5	+1.7
5	2.1	4.3	+2.2
6	2.4	4.0	+1.6
7	1.4	4.1	+2.7
8	2.8	3.9	+1.1
9	1.3	3.2	+1.9
10	1.5	4.8	+3.3

FIGURE **9**_____

Calculating the Mean for Group Members' Responses on Item 1

Group Member	Numerical Score
Paul	4
Ida	3
Mike	4
Phil	1
Ena	2
Frank	3
Lori	2
Cathy	4
	Total 23 divided by 8 = 2.87
	(rounded to 2.9)

A positive number in the "Difference" column suggests an attitudinal change for the whole group in the expected and hoped-for direction—that is, toward a more mentally healthy attitude. A negative number suggests a change in the opposite direction.

Once you obtain data from a pretest and posttest, you have the option of reporting this information to individual children, in order to help them understand where they stand after the group, and/or reporting the evaluation results of the group as a whole, without using individual names. Group data can be shared with administrators, evaluators, or parents to indicate whether group members' attitudes have changed in the direction of healthier attitudes or beliefs (or skills, if that is what is being measured). It is important to be clear about who owns the data, what should be done with it, who may have access to it, and how it will be stored. All data should be kept confidential, with access limited to the professional counselor. Keep in mind, however, that the Buckley Amendment allows parents to have access to their children's records and the courts could subpoena counseling records.

Assessing Leader Effectiveness

Another important area of accountability concerns leader effectiveness. A self-evaluation checklist like the one shown in Figure 10 can help you identify your strengths as well as areas in which you need to improve. (The checklist is not all inclusive; adapt as necessary for your situation.)

Step 5: Accomplishing the Selection Process

Interviewing Prospective Members

The ethical guidelines of our counseling specialty require us to screen potential members for a group so that we may obtain informed consent (or, in the case of minors, assent). We also need to ascertain the child's level of commitment to the group and obtain other information that will help in deciding to admit the child to the group. Even though it is a lengthy process, interviewing prospective group members is important because, as noted in the discussion of ethical and professional issues, group counseling has the potential to be harmful under certain conditions. It is our responsibility to check out potential problems and screen out children who are not appropriate candidates.

Screening may be accomplished in several ways. For example, you could conduct an individual interview. Another method often used is to share basic information in a small group of potential members and then meet more briefly with individuals. A third option, frequently the method in inpatient or outpatient treatment centers, involves having the treatment team meet to discuss possible candidates for a particular group. Yet another way to screen is for the potential member to be given a written questionnaire covering information about the group and asking for specific responses.

The best of all possible methods, in my judgment, is the individual interview. This affords a better opportunity for privacy and disclosure on the child's part as well as for you to focus in on that child to get a reading on his or her suitability for the group. The TAP-In Selection Checklist (see Appendix B) can help you structure the information to be presented and obtained. In using this checklist, it is important to talk with the child for a while to develop rapport and to tell the child that he or she is being interviewed for a place in the group. Tell the child that being in the group is very special, that only a few children will be selected, and

Figure **10**

Leader Effectiveness Checklist

Scale

    1 = very satisfied

    2 = satisfied

    3 = unsatisfied/needs work

    4 = must change/improve before next group

Preparation

_____ 1. Overall topic suitable to children's needs at this time.

_____ 2. Sequence of session topics seems appropriate.

_____ 3. Proposal accomplished intended purpose.

_____ 4. Method(s) of advertising group were effective.

_____ 5. Consent process was adequate.

_____ 6. Pregroup interview process worked effectively.

_____ 7. Selection/rejection process was adequate.

_____ 8. Time and resources were allotted effectively.

_____ 9. Indirectly related persons were prepared effectively.

_____ 10. Evaluation process and instrument(s) chosen
were adequate.

_____ 11. Pretest administration system worked effectively.

Leadership during Group

_____ 1. Each session provided time for ice breaker or review
of previous session and "homework."

_____ 2. Each session had clear transitions from review time
to working time to process time.

_____ 3. Working time allowed all members to participate
actively in some way.

_____ 4. Activities or exercises were developmentally appropriate.

Figure 10 (continued)

_____ 5. Activities or exercises were appropriate in terms of affect.

_____ 6. Activities or exercises were appropriate in length/time allowed.

_____ 7. Confidentiality was explained/stressed during each session.

_____ 8. Each child was encouraged and taught how to set appropriate personal goals for the group.

_____ 9. Linking was used each session to build group cohesion.

_____ 10. Distinctions between thinking, feeling, and behaving were taught at the beginning and reinforced throughout the group's life.

_____ 11. Empathy statements were used with each child during each session.

_____ 12. Open-ended questions were used instead of closed-ended questions.

_____ 13. Problematic or difficult situations with group members were used as learning experiences for leader and members.

_____ 14. Children were allowed and encouraged to express negative as well as positive emotions.

_____ 15. Cutting-off skills were used effectively and in a timely manner.

_____ 16. Drawing-out skills were used effectively and in a timely manner.

_____ 17. Focusing skills were used to maximize the group experience.

_____ 18. Dyads or other mini-group formats were used effectively.

_____ 19. Go-arounds were carried through so everyone who wanted to respond could do so.

_____ 20. Any strong emotions expressed were handled effectively.

_____ 21. The individuality of each child was respected without regard to race, sex, ability, nationality, culture, and so forth.

_____ 22. No favoritism or prejudice was shown toward any group member.

_____ 23. Sufficient process time was set aside for each session.

_____ 24. Between-session self-improvement homework was encouraged.

_____ 25. Homework was selected and/or clearly understood and agreed to by group members.

_____ 26. Children were equally reinforced for attempts to change behaviors, for practice of new behaviors, and for accomplished behavior change.

_____ 27. Children were not allowed to leave the group session in obvious emotional upset or pain.

_____ 28. Children were reminded that they could "pass" on activities or questions they found uncomfortable.

_____ 29. Reminders were given that the group would be ending two to three sessions before the last session.

_____ 30. The last session gave closure to the experience and reviewed what was learned.

Postgroup Experiences

_____ 1. Posttest administered 2 to 4 weeks after the last session.

_____ 2. Children had the opportunity to give the leader feedback about what they learned, as well as liked and disliked about the group.

_____ 3. Referrals were made in a timely manner for children who needed continued help.

_____ 4. Evaluation procedure was completed, written into document, shared with group members, and added to counseling program annual review information.

_____ 5. Follow-up session was scheduled for 1 month after last session for review and support of group members.

Figure 10 (continued)

> Review the numbers assigned to the previous questions.
> Describe plans to make changes for any items that need
> work or improvement before the next group.

Preparation

_____

_____

_____

_____

_____

Leadership during Group

_____

_____

_____

_____

Postgroup Experiences

_____

_____

_____

_____

_____

that parent permission is required. Tell the child that you will need to share a number of things, ask some questions, and write the information down so you can remember it.

Generally speaking, the younger the child and/or the more severe the problems, the more important it is to have an individual selection interview. Children frequently feel inhibited to share in front of others and might not give the counselor important information needed to make a selection decision if others are present. If an individual interview is not realistic, a small-group interview session can be effective, depending on the setting, the topics to be discussed, and the severity of the problems.

Obtaining Parent/Guardian Consent

In many schools, parents or legal guardians must provide a written informed consent in order for minor children to participate in group counseling. Other schools consider group participation as part of the regular curriculum offered to youth attending that school, and thus permission is not necessary. Service agencies obtain permission in a variety of ways. When permission is advisable or necessary, specific information needs to be provided about the group so that the child and the parent/guardian can make an intelligent decision about whether or not to participate. Cormier and Cormier (1991) have developed a general checklist for informed consent that incorporates the following points:

1. Description of each strategy, including activities involved

2. Rationale for or purpose of the strategy

3. Description of the counselor's role

4. Description of the client's role

5. Description of possible risks or discomforts

6. Description of expected benefits

7. Offer made to answer client's questions about strategy

8. Client advisement of the right to discontinue strategy at any time

9. Explanations in clear and nontechnical language

10. Summary and/or clarifications to explore and understand client reactions

The importance of obtaining informed consent from the parent/ guardian, as well as assent from the child, cannot be overstated. One good way to provide the necessary information is to develop a consent form. Figure 11 shows a sample form used to obtain consent in a school setting.

Check your agency or school policy on consent from both custodial and noncustodial parents before making any final selection of members. Many parents have joint legal custody, with the child living primarily with one parent. Both parents should receive information about the prospective group experience if both make decisions about the child's welfare. It might not be advisable to select a child who does not have the permission of both parents. A parent's objection may influence or become a source of confusion for the child, resulting in the child's inability to participate fully or dropping out of the group.

Administering the Pretest

You can administer your pretest in a number of different ways. For example, if you have 15 youths who appear to be candidates for the group, you can use the pretest along with other criteria to select the 8 you believe would work best in the group. In this way you can select some low scorers and some high scorers on a particular dimension. If you are not using pretest results as part of the selection criteria, you can interview the prospective members, select for the group, and then pretest the selected members before the first session.

Selecting Group Members

A great deal of controversy exists in the field about which children are best suited for group counseling. The research in this area has been conducted on adult therapy groups, with little or no definitive guidelines for children and adolescents. The ideas for achieving an ideal balance presented here reflect my own two decades of experience in group work with children and adolescents.

When selecting members for a group, the principle of homogeneity/heterogeneity will help you select members that are more likely to "work" in the group. *Homogeneity* means selection on the basis of likenesses, such as all children whose families have experienced a divorce, or a loss of a loved one, or are experiencing problems managing anger. It also means likenesses in terms of intellectual level, grade level, socioeconomic status, cultural background, and so forth. Homogeneity has certain benefits and limitations in a group.

FIGURE **11** _____

Sample Parent/Guardian Consent Form

Your permission is requested for your child, _____ ,
to participate in group counseling activities. The group will
involve eight sessions and will run from _____ to_____.
Each session will be about _____ minutes long and will take place
during the school day.

The group is entitled _____
and will include discussion of ideas, feelings, behaviors, attitudes,
and opinions. The children will do some activities related to the
topic, such as drawing, role-playing, relaxation exercises, and
practicing new behaviors both in group and between sessions with
family members and friends. For example, your child could be
practicing telling you how she or he feels about a related issue.

Some of the session topics are:

_____
_____
_____

The children will have the opportunity to learn new skills and
behaviors that may help their personal development and adjustment.
The group will be led by _____ of the school counseling staff.

Because counseling is based on a trusting relationship between
counselor and client, the group leader(s) will keep the information
shared by group members confidential, except in certain situations
in which there is an ethical responsibility to limit confidentiality. In
the following circumstances you will be notified.

1. If the child reveals information about harm to himself/herself
   or another person

2. If the child reveals information about child abuse

3. If the counselor's records are subpoenaed by the courts

4. Other _____

Figure 11 (continued)

By signing this form I give my informed consent for my child to participate in group counseling. I understand that:

1. The group will provide an opportunity for members to learn and practice interpersonal skills, discuss feelings, share ideas, practice new behaviors, and make new friends.

2. Anything group members share in group will be kept confidential by the group leader(s) except in the situations already noted.

Parent/Guardian _____ Date _____

Parent/Guardian _____ Date _____

Student _____ Date _____

Return to _____ By _____

Benefits

The group seems to "gel" or develop cohesion faster.

The group offers more immediate support to group members and seems to be attended more regularly.

More rapid relief of symptoms takes place.

The group reflects a sense of commonality (universality) in working on shared or similar problems.

Limitations

Too much likeness presents less opportunity to learn new behaviors.

Interactions among group members seem more superficial.

Too much similarity inhibits healthy conflict.

Less opportunity to appreciate differences exists.

Selection for homogeneity appears to be better for certain problems and situations. For example, short-term topic-driven groups in a school setting seem to work well when children are selected who have similar problems, such as dealing with a family divorce, transition to a new setting, or self-esteem issues. In agency or other settings, youths who have all experienced issues such as drug or alcohol abuse appear to feel a more immediate connection with other youths who have struggled or are struggling with the same issues.

Heterogeneity refers to the differences among group members— for example, different social or cultural backgrounds, differences in attitudes and coping skills for a particular problem, or different stages of dealing with an issue. Heterogeneity as a basis for member selection has its benefits and limitations also.

Benefits

The group provides a variety of opinions and new ideas.

Role models for different behaviors exist.

The group provides the opportunity for valuable feedback from those with different perceptions.

The group offers opportunities to correct distorted perceptions of self and others.

Limitations

It usually takes more time for benefits of the group experience to occur.

The group usually takes longer to become cohesive (generally longer than most school settings provide).

Frequently, there will be more conflict in the beginning because members don't "relate" as quickly.

The most important advice in selecting group members in terms of homogeneity/heterogeneity seems to be *role balance*. Because the beauty and power of group work comes from members influencing one another, each member needs to be a role model in some way for the other members. Each group member is also entitled to have other members from whom he or she can learn new behaviors, attitudes, coping skills, and ways of thinking. The role balance rule is the most important aspect of member selection.

Choose members who are homogeneous for certain aspects and heterogeneous for other aspects. Homogeneity can be reflected in your topical basis, as in a group of teenage mothers; heterogeneity can be expressed in terms of their coping skills in dealing with being a teen mom, attitudes toward furthering their education, ability to deal with dating and relationships, and so forth. Each young woman in such a group will be able to relate to the others because they all share the same issue, and each can learn new and more adaptive ways of dealing with related problems. Another example would be to choose children whose families have experienced divorce (homogeneity) but who are heterogeneous in terms of length of time since the divorce, their coping strategies, attitudes toward divorce and stepfamilies, and new family constellations. In creating a group of children who all have problems with anger, you could create a heterogeneous role balance by choosing two or three children who act out their anger, one or two who act in their anger, one or two who have used their angry energy to excel in sports, and one or two who have used their angry energy to excel in music or academics. You would not want to choose all children who act out their anger, or the group will not include any role models for group members to learn other ways to deal with anger. Such a group can quickly deteriorate into an us-against-them situation in which the adult group leader attempts to convince the youths that there are more appropriate ways to behave.

In addition to the homogeneity/heterogeneity issue, there are some other general guidelines for selection of members.

Do select

A range of participants so each child will have at least one positive behavioral model

Children who are not more than 2 years apart chronologically

Children with approximately the same social, emotional, intellectual, and physical maturity

Children who respond well to social influence

Children who are known to be able to work cooperatively in a group situation

Children from different racial, cultural, ethnic and socio-economic backgrounds

Both boys and girls (unless the topic is inappropriate or would cause one sex to be uncomfortable—e.g., a group for pregnant girls)

Do not select

Siblings or relatives who might feel they have to adhere to familial roles or expectations within the group or that their confidences would not be safe

Children who are suicidal or homicidal or who have seriously considered attempting these actions

Children who are involved in ongoing sexual activity (heterosexual or homosexual) if such behavior is exceptional within the group

Children who habitually lie or steal

Children who are in a recent or ongoing crisis (unless the group is specifically designed to deal with this issue)

Children whom you know or strongly suspect are being physically or sexually abused (unless this is the topic of the group and you are prepared to deal with it)

Children whose parents are divided against having the child participate

Children who are too "different" from the rest of the group (e.g., one pregnant girl or one new student from Vietnam who has not yet fully adjusted)

Children who are extremely aggressive, either physically or verbally

After reading this list, you might think that all of your young clients have just been eliminated! Many settings deal with an entire population with serious problems who all need to learn more adaptive social skills. Group can be a wonderful place for them to learn. But the previously mentioned issues present special challenges. For example, children with many of these issues (the suicidal child, the child in a recent crisis, the child who lies and steals for attention, or the child who is being abused) are so overwhelmed emotionally that they can be extremely demanding of group time and the counselor's attention. Such children cannot be positive role models for other group members because the current emotional crisis saps their psychological energy. If you are in a setting where you have unlimited time and resources to work with a child on some of these overwhelming issues, perhaps they will do well in a group. But in most cases, group work is more suited for children whose psychological needs are equally balanced.

In some inpatient settings, it seems to be regular practice to include all patients who are there at the time, whether they are suited to the group experience or not. If you are required by agency policy to see all clients in group, some adjustments can be made. First, be sure to educate administrators on the ethical responsibilities of group leadership. Once made aware of ethical group practice, many administrators will be open to having that agency's business conducted in an ethical and professional manner for the benefit of clients and to avoid legal problems. If there does not seem to be a way to be more flexible on screening out inappropriate members, you can request flexibility on size of the group and/or frequency of meetings. For example, if there are 12 children on the unit and all of them must be seen in group, have three shorter group experiences with four members in each group, or make some other arrangement that improves their chances of profiting from group. If you must accept a child who is not suited for the experience, you will need to make whatever adjustments you can. Less control on the selection of appropriate members nearly always results in a less-than-optimum experience for both leader and members.

Sometimes counselors have difficulty explaining to teachers, administrators, or parents why a child who seems to have a great need for counseling services might not be a good group member. One way to explain this is to use the following analogy: Suppose you decide you would like to have cosmetic surgery. You choose a reputable surgeon, make an appointment, and discuss what you would like to have done. Before putting you on the list for the operation, the surgeon will send you for a series of tests to obtain information on your suitability as a candidate for surgery. If you are a suitable candidate, then you may find yourself getting ready to go under the knife. If results indicate that for some reason you are not an appropriate candidate, you will be informed that it would not be in your best interests to proceed. It is the same way with group counseling: Some children are simply not suitable candidates for group counseling. They may need more intense counseling than the diluted attention given in a group, or they may be in a personal crisis and not work well in a group situation.

Step 6: Preparing Resources

Group work with children requires an extra effort to coordinate the materials needed for the sessions. Children's developmental ages and stages differ, and play rather than "talk therapy" is their natural medium for communication. Play therapy has been used successfully in both individual and group work with children, especially young children. As Dr. JoAnna White, expert in the field of play therapy and group work, points out, "Play therapy is a developmentally appropriate approach for school counselors to take with the children that they work with on an individual basis and in small group work. Because of their developmental level, small children cannot express their feelings and concerns verbally. However, they can work through their emotional needs with play materials in a safe environment. This play serves as a metaphor for the child's life at that time" (personal communication, May 31, 1994). Many excellent resources on play therapy exist (e.g., Allen, 1979; Axline, 1947; O'Connor, 1991; Witmer & Young, 1987).

You will need to have on hand a supply of materials suited to helping children and adolescents communicate through play and creative arts—for example, drawing/painting materials, puppets, music, dance/movement activities, films/filmstrips/videos, acting/dress-up props, and written material such as books, poetry, charts/lists/paperwork. These materials need to be prepared in advance so that they are ready for the session. For example, certain supplies might be low, such as art paper or markers, or you might need to send for a book for the bibliotherapy part of a session. If you are using the *Skills for Living* series (Morganett, 1990, 1994) to conduct a group on a particular topic, check the list of materials suggested for each session and obtain the resources for the session. Preread or preview all materials to be used so that you can maximize their use. If you are using duplicated handouts, try to set aside some time before the group starts to make the copies for each session; file them so you are prepared and don't have to make them at the last minute.

In addition to preparing materials, you will need to give some thought to contacting any individuals or groups who will be affected by the sessions. These "human resources" have a strong impact on the emotional tone of the group's environment. First, if you are in an inpatient or school setting where youths will be coming directly from a class or activity into the group setting, you will need to prepare the adults who work with these children so they can help children get to group on time. These individuals, as well as those who conduct classes or activities immediately following the group, must know when sessions will be held and that it is unacceptable to interrupt the session unless it is truly an emergency. You can convey this information by talking with them and/or giving them a note beforehand, briefly outlining your thoughts or "policy" on how you feel about the group. In this note you could reiterate that group members' disclosures are kept confidential within the limits of confidentiality (harm-abuse-courts), express your appreciation for their respecting your belief in the importance of not disturbing the group for any reason other than an emergency, and thank them for their cooperation and interest in the children.

Parents or guardians of the children participating in the group also need to be clear about what is likely to happen in group. This can be done in a letter that accompanies the consent form, stating the topics to be discussed, describing some of the techniques to be used, and, again, clarifying the limits of confidentiality. Regarding the issue of child abuse reporting, it is recommended that you state in your letter that if the child's disclosures need to be reported, the parent will be notified. In states where reports of child abuse must be made directly to the child protective services department, that agency, not you, will be the one to inform the parents.

If there are persons in your agency or school such as administrators, administrative assistants, secretaries, practicum/internship students, and so forth, you will need to make them aware of the times group sessions will be held so anyone who needs to be there is on time and does not inadvertently disturb the group while it is in session. Sometimes others are not aware of how important it is for the group to have privacy and how deeply an interruption can affect children who have just developed the trust to work on their issues. So use your assertive skills, let others know in advance not to interrupt, and hang a sign on the door reminding others not to enter!

Step 7: Conducting the Sessions

As you prepare for the group, you will need to consider a number of issues relating to session agenda, group size, scheduling, and the meeting area.

The Session Agenda

One of the ways to keep a handle on the time for the session is to divide the session time into sections, each devoted to a major task:

1. Ice-breaker or review

2. Working time

3. Process time

The ice breaker or review time and the process time should be about one-quarter of the total group time; the remaining half should be devoted to the working time. (The sample session outline shown in Figure 4 illustrates this way of structuring the group meeting.)

The very first time your group meets, you will need to have an ice breaker (also called boundary breaker) activity. This is a planned activity to get the members acquainted with one other, begin setting norms, and help members understand the types of things that will happen during the group. Because it is so critical to getting off to a positive start, this activity might take longer than one-quarter of the session. Even if group members already know one another, it is important to do some activity to help them understand that group is not the same as play or school and that the relationships developed in group are different.

After the first session, each and every session will begin with review time. In this part, it is important to begin by asking the children if they have any "old business"—any ideas, feelings, thoughts, or questions about what happened in the session before. By establishing a connection with the joys, pains, and learning experiences of the previous session, you create a link between all of the sessions and help children realize that the group experience is not just a single event. Another important function of review time is to share about what children might have practiced during the time between sessions. Group work is about change, and if the children are working on self-improvement homework between sessions, it is up to you to create an opportunity for them to talk about their changes and attempts at change. If you ask them to practice or try some new behavior and forget to bring it up at the next session, they will be highly unlikely to try.

The working time, the longest part of the group session, concentrates on the topic or the individual(s) who are the focus of the group that day. This part of the group takes the major portion of time. Its content varies with the group topic, development, and purpose.

The process time is actually the most important part of the session because it allows group members to focus on what they have felt and learned and to formulate plans for working on behavior changes to be practiced between sessions. The beauty of group work is that each member learns from all of the other members, as well as from the leader, so the process time is a critical aspect of this learning experience.

Group Size

For children at the elementary level, the recommended number of students for a group counseling experience is six to eight. This number is, of course, the ideal, and it is possible to have a successful group experience with fewer or more participants. However, six to eight seems to be a good range because it allows for a variety of ideas and behaviors and permits you to let students form dyads for specific activities. If there are more than eight, the students who are less inclined to self-disclose tend not to be heard. Fewer than about six children means that the time will be concentrated on only those children: Some children cannot tolerate the pressure of constantly sharing and disclosing. There will also be fewer ideas and viewpoints to be shared.

Scheduling

Most group counseling experiences for children and adolescents will be comparatively short term—perhaps 8 to 12 sessions. In terms of group counseling, this is a very small number of sessions to have expectations for permanent behavioral change—the best that can be hoped for is some attitudinal change. Some children will change behavior, but you should not expect long-term change in ingrained maladaptive behaviors.

You can schedule the sessions to occur once per week, if that suits your school or agency's schedule, or you can schedule them twice weekly. The latter option works just as well for many groups. Some topical areas that include practice on skills for behavior change may require a week between sessions for practice to occur. Having the sessions more than twice weekly is not recommended unless you are working in an inpatient setting. Be sure to check the school calendar before you schedule the group so that there are no weeks the group cannot meet. For trust and cohesion to develop, continuity is essential.

The length of the sessions may vary according to your daily schedule. If you are working with younger children, ages 6 through 8 years, a 30-minute session would be appropriate. For ages 9 through 13, a 40- to 45-minute session works well. For youths over age 13, a 45- to 60-minute session is appropriate, if the setting allows.

In groups conducted in a school setting, parents, teachers, and children often express concern about missing a particular academic subject to attend group. This issue is especially important when a child is already having academic difficulty and then has to miss a class periodically to attend group. You might want to vary the time the group is held so children do not miss the same subject each time they attend. One way to deal with this is to have group first period/hour in the morning one week, second period/hour the next week, and so on. If you have an activity period when all of the children are available, this would be ideal. Whatever you do, try to avoid putting the child at further risk for academic problems and distress.

The Meeting Area

Confidentiality is a major issue in all group counseling, and ensuring that children have a place where they will feel comfortable disclosing without someone overhearing will help them develop a feeling of security. Choose a room that closes completely and be sure you hang a sign on the door reminding people not to enter during the session unless there is an emergency. It is up to you to set the tone and let others know how important the issue of privacy is to group counseling.

You will need enough chairs, cushions, pillows, or bean-bag chairs for you and all group members to be able to sit in a circle. Do not sit around a table because the table will distract the children and serve as a barrier. Be sure that each child in the group can see you and every other child clearly. You will need to have a table or some other flat surface available for drawing, a chalkboard or some kind of flip chart to write on occasionally, a box for puppets and drawing materials, and, of course, a box of tissues! It is not recommended that you take the group outside or to other places where there will be many distractions unless doing so serves a specific purpose in the session.

Step 8: Administering the Posttest

After the last session of the group experience, you will want to administer the same measures used as the pretest to evaluate possible changes in ideas, attitudes, and behaviors. Since children change and learn so much in short periods of time, it is important not to wait more than 2 to 3 weeks before collecting this information; if you do, you increase the chance that you are really measuring maturation and learning from other sources, thus contaminating your results.

You can ask each group member to stop by your office for a few minutes to take the posttest, or you can administer the posttest when you meet during the postgroup follow-up session, discussed in the next section. Do not use the last session for the posttest; it is important to use that time to process what happened in the previous sessions, to say good-bye, and to celebrate the learning that took place with the other group members.

It is also a good idea to develop and administer some type of questionnaire to gather information on how the children perceived you as a leader during the group experience. If we are willing to be models for youth, then we need to be willing to take feedback and improve our own performance and increase our skills, just as we require that they do.

Step 9: Completing the Evaluation Procedure

When the posttests have been scored and other verbal or written feedback gathered, the information will need to be written up in a brief report describing the experience in general and giving a pretest-posttest comparison (see Step 4, on developing an accountability strategy).

Remember that these data belong to the children, and their names should be kept confidential when reporting the results. Only in extreme circumstances may individual scores be shared, and only with parental permission and the child's assent. The information obtained can be used for the following purposes:

For reporting to agency or school administrators, parents, teachers, probation officers/court system, or funding sources on the direction of change that may have occurred in the group as a result of participation

To compare pretest and posttest responses for each member to help that member achieve behavior change goals

To obtain an idea of the group leader's effectiveness

To assist the group leader in planning for his or her own skill improvement in the future

To become part of the evaluation data for the counseling service program

Step 10: Conducting the Postgroup Follow-Up Session

Approximately 4 to 6 weeks after the end of the group, it is appropriate to reconvene the group members for a brief session to allow them to share their accomplishments and perceptions of what happened in the group, as well as the progress and problems related to the practice of their new skills, behaviors, and attitudes. They will also need encouragement and support to continue with any behavioral changes they have made. Sometimes members do well for a few weeks after the group but lose touch with the new skills and need a refresher to motivate and recharge. They are usually happy to get together again and cheer each other on, give support and suggestions, report on their successes, and get supportive feedback on their growth areas.

Understanding Group Process

The interpersonal forces that cause the tug and push among members of any group or in any relationship are called *dynamics*, the "magical glue" of groups. The most important group dynamic in this context is that of trust, which must develop and grow among the group membership. Without trust there is no involvement, movement, or growth because members will not feel comfortable enough to self-disclose and work on their problems. The children in your group will have different trust levels depending on their previous experiences in relationships. Because the population for a group experience is one in which the members already have issues that have become problematic, it is likely that some will lack trust in this new situation. Be patient when you encounter resistance—or as Virginia Satir called it at one family therapy conference, "justified caution"—in your young members. Use your modeling skills to develop trust. Trust yourself and the group process and bring issues out in the open as they occur to prevent hidden agendas from developing. Be aware that trust develops slowly and must be nurtured and encouraged.

Another important dynamic that works to bond the group is a sense of cohesion, or "we-ness." Cohesion also develops slowly, as the group members take risks to share themselves and their hurt, anger, painful experiences, and efforts at healing. In the beginning of the group there exist only individuals; the sense of being a group with a purpose is not yet present. Group cohesion can be nurtured but grows only after members share activities, reveal feelings, undergo and work out problems, and discover that they have painful experiences in common. When cohesion develops, you will be able to sense a spirit of cooperation in the group, shared pleasure in one another's accomplishments, and a willingness to continue sharing and undertaking self-improvement activities.

The group experience unfolds over time as members go through the process of learning to trust, self-disclose, and grow. This process occurs as stages or phases with identifiable behaviors marking them. Many researchers have studied these stages, common to all groups. Tuckman (Tuckman, 1965; Tuckman & Jensen, 1977) calls these stages forming, storming, norming, performing, and adjourning. Corey and Corey (1992) identify initial, transition, working, and final stages.

The following discussion presents some guidelines for group work with children and adolescents as they apply to the various group stages, with Corey and Corey's formulation of the group stages as its basis. To Corey and Corey's schema I have added a stage that precedes the initial stage, the pregroup stage. The "Do's and Don'ts" presented here reflect suggested practice rather than inviolable standards. Many of these suggestions involve use of the leadership and therapeutic interaction skills described in Sections 2 and 3 of this book—for example, linking, drawing out, "I" statements, processing, and so forth. For more information about these skills, please refer to those specific sections.

Pregroup Stage

The pregroup stage is the stage before the group even begins. Your planning and organization at this point will have a profound impact on how the group experience unfolds.

Do

1. Choose a pleasant room for group counseling, large enough for members to be comfortable in both seated and active situations, but not so large that young children could wander off or become involved with books, materials, or computers also stored in the room.

2. Provide comfortable chairs, bean-bag chairs, rugs, or a comforter for the children to sit on. Let them choose where and how they want to sit.

3. Select a room or area for group that ensures confidentiality.

4. Develop a method to call or have younger children brought to the group room at the appropriate time, if applicable.

5. Prepare materials and post-group snacks, if used, before the session, and have everything ready so as not to waste session time with logistics.

6. Prepare and hang a sign on the door stating that group is not to be disturbed except for emergencies; relate this information to others in your setting—the faculty, staff, and so on.

Don't

1. Have the children sit at a table; this creates a distracting psychological barrier and keeps them from connecting with one another.

2. Answer the phone, door, or allow others to walk in and interrupt the session; this disturbs the children's privacy and teaches others in the environment that you do not mean what you say when you ask for client privacy.

3. Expect children to understand the norms and expectations (taking turns, self-disclosing, reinforcing one another, practicing new behaviors, not raising your hand to speak, etc.) of the group experience without your modeling and reinforcing the behaviors many times.

4. Expect the children to understand the difference between thoughts, feelings, and behaviors without being taught.

5. Expect young children to do talk therapy; both children and adolescents profit from activities and exercises to stimulate discussion and transfer of learning.

Initial Stage

During this stage, children's behavior reflects their confusion about the nature of groups and their anxiety in resolving the following issues:

Developing a safe, trusting environment for self-disclosure

Being accepted by the others as a group member

Figuring out what group is all about and what the "rules of the game" are (i.e., understanding norms)

Making efforts to please the leader and other members

Meeting new children and beginning to develop alliances

Do

1. Start the first session by having a carefully designed ice-breaker activity to help the children get acquainted in a positive way.

2. Use linking skills from the very beginning, having the children say whom they connected with after the ice-breaker.

3. Remind group members of the confidentiality rule and the limits of confidentiality. (Using a chart like the one shown in Figure 2 can help illustrate the limits.)

4. Discuss how the group is going to deal with the breaking of confidentiality by group members; let them decide.

5. Discuss the ground rules. State the ones you have decided on and give members input into developing others as needed.

6. Begin teaching the norms desired in the group—for example, self-disclosing, taking turns talking, and talking directly to one another instead of to you as the leader.

7. Use drawing-out skills as necessary to try to get every child to speak at least once during each session.

8. Clearly reinforce appropriate self-disclosures and attempts at sharing feelings.

9. Ask the group openly and directly about how they are feeling about trusting the group, if they are lacking trust, and what they need to develop or keep on building trust.

10. Encourage the children to practice new behaviors tried out in group between the sessions.

11. Establish the habit of saving enough time at the end of the session to process what happened and ask for commitments to do self-improvement homework between sessions.

12. Respect and understand that resistant children are usually afraid and insecure. Go slowly and let them come along as they warm up to the experience and find out they are safe; tell them openly that it is OK to be cautious because it is a little scary getting used to the group.

13. Dyads work well for the first session or two for introductory experiences because it is easier for group members to talk to one other member than to talk to the whole group; however, be careful not to overdo dyads.

14. End the session with praise and thanks for children's sharing; if appropriate, give them a healthy snack such as boxes of raisins or fruit as a reinforcer and an opportunity to talk informally.

Don't

1. Let the time get away from you; be sure to have clear, smooth transitions from ice breaker/review to working time and from working time to process time.

2. Allow children to begin monopolizing, story-telling, or taking up group time with unrelated events or information; use cutting-off skills and redirect or refocus so they know you want them to stay on the topic.

3. Allow children to pick on, tease, ridicule, or pressure other children; stop these behaviors immediately and discuss why you are doing so.

4. Pressure children to participate or self-disclose if they are afraid or don't have the skills—employ patience, modeling, patience, reinforcement, patience!

5. Use too long or complicated of an ice-breaker that takes up the working time during the first session. Remember that you also need to cover confidentiality and ground rules during the first session.

6. Overuse exercises or let activities take the place of the natural group dynamics. Use exercises according to the developmental level of the children and only to enhance the group goals.

7. Use a "teacher voice" in group; instead, use your voice to develop a more personal (relaxed, genuine) atmosphere so children will understand that group is different than class—that is, process versus content oriented.

8. Let the session end without thanking group members and reminding them of the time, place, and requirements for the next meeting.

Transition Stage

In group work with children, this stage takes a somewhat different form than in adult groups. Unless they have an extreme lack of trust as a result of early traumatic life experiences, children tend to move more quickly toward the working stage than adults do. During this stage, major behaviors revolve around these characteristic issues:

Assessment of the leader's personal care and concern

Assessment of the leader's ability to help with problems

Deciding if the group is a safe place to disclose more than superficial feelings

Learning and testing the waters to decide if feedback can be given and accepted

Clarifying what goals are and how to go about working on them

Clarifying what feelings and thoughts are and how to share thoughts and feelings without being overly anxious or inhibited

Awareness that other children have problems, too

Awareness of the need to develop connections with others who have similar problems

Do

1. Be supportive and reinforcing of children who express negative thoughts and feelings (as well as positive feelings).

2. Help members clarify what they want to accomplish during the group. Setting clear goals helps make the group meaningful by engendering a sense of hope that the goals can be accomplished.

3. Encourage a sense of "we-ness," or cohesion, by pointing out connections when the group seems to be on the same wavelength.

4. Provide learning experiences so members can acquire and practice skills in the group, gain confidence, and be encouraged to practice outside of group.

5. Model being "real," not phony, by self-disclosing appropriately, being willing to be honest about children's feelings and behaviors, accepting children as they are, and gently encouraging them to make changes.

6. Use gentle confrontation to help children look at any inconsistencies in what they are wanting, doing, and feeling. For example, say, "On the one hand you really want to make something of yourself

and get a good education, but on the other hand it looks like you keep sabotaging your goal by doing things to get in trouble and make low grades. What do you think might be keeping you from reaching your goal?"

7. If hostile behaviors erupt, deal directly with them. Ask hostile children what it is like to be in a group where they don't want to be or what it is like for them to have a lot of anger inside them.

8. Help children take responsibility for their own behaviors and feelings by asking them to replace "he or she made me feel" with "I chose to feel."

9. Encourage each child to make a plan for ways to start or increase certain behaviors and to change, decrease, or eliminate other behaviors.

Don't

1. Deny, avoid, or try to repress negative interactions in the group. At this stage, it is critical for the children to observe how you deal with acting-out behavior, breeches of confidentiality, anger and hostility, and power struggles. Leader modeling of appropriate behaviors is extremely important at this point.

2. Avoid dealing with conflicts that arise between children in the group. When different ideas, values, beliefs, or attitudes begin to be expressed, use this as an opportunity to teach children that it is OK to have different ideas on an issue by bringing the conflicting opinions out into the open.

3. Avoid dealing with "hidden agendas," or covert feelings or behaviors that can affect the progress of the group. Examples include a member's need to be in the limelight, to be invited several times to participate, or to control the leader.

4. Avoid dealing with common fears of group participation, such as the following: "Other group members won't like me"; "I can't do anything about this situation, so why bother?"; "I don't have any feelings"; or "I think I'll drop out of group because it's boring."

5. Use too many activities and/or exercises that take away from the natural group process. Instead, tolerate group members' frustration as they learn to self-disclose and work together. Be calm, helping them work through conflicts so that all members can learn to trust and work.

6. Let confidentiality breaks go without dealing with this issue in group. Discuss the situation and let the group decide how to deal with it, in conjunction with previously set ground rules.

7. Give up on the group! Have patience and let members come along slowly; keep modeling being a reinforcing person, linking members, and letting members become involved as they feel comfortable.

Working Stage

The working stage is characterized by such behaviors and situations as the following:

Children's coming to group saying that they are practicing the new skills and behaviors they learned in the group in other situations—for example, managing anger in better ways, being assertive with a bully, meeting new friends, following a plan to stay out of trouble in class, and so forth

Children's following the norms set in the group to share equally, listen to one another, and be supportive of other children's attempts at new behaviors and progress. At this stage members also connect with one another, are cooperative and work together in a cohesive manner, express positive and negative feelings, and are able to add to the processing time at the end of the session with somewhat insightful responses

Children's ability to be more immediate and deal with the here-and-now context of things that happen in the group

Children's ability to articulate their plans and goals and tell what they are working on and why

Children's ability to ask for help from other group members and profit from feedback

It is important to help the group move toward the working stage, but you also need to realize that this is a very advanced stage of group work, and some time-limited, topic driven groups do not reach this point. Frequently, the number of sessions is just too few to bring about the dynamic process of interaction. Sometimes children are unable to deal with intense issues in a short period of time, and the knowledge that the time is limited keeps them from becoming more involved. Some may become involved and rake up raw feelings only to have insufficient time to resolve them. Others just don't know how to get in touch with and let go of feelings and would require more intense therapy and an extended group experience to do so.

Do

1. Continue to be a model and reinforce attempts at behavior change and practice of more positive behaviors.

2. Challenge members to practice new skills and express new attitudes outside as well as inside the group.

3. Continue to build trust by keeping communication open, acknowledging conflicts, and dealing with intense feelings.

4. Allow children to cry or experience negative feelings without "rescuing" and encourage them to connect with one another to teach the value of networking and support.

5. If the group has a specific number of sessions, give frequent reminders in advance of the group's ending so members who want to bring up issues will know that they need to do so and so everyone will realize the group will be saying good-bye at some point.

6. Confront members in a positive way so that they learn to confront themselves and experience this type of invitation as a stimulus to keep on working on the problems and behaviors they need to change.

7. Be aware that some cultural groups do not value self-disclosure and realize that movement toward sharing is very difficult for some children to achieve, even if they are in the process of changing their beliefs.

8. Keep reinforcing the need to take personal responsibility for behavior, helping each child change "you" statements to "I" statements.

9. Give specific feedback in an immediate manner, without collecting negative feelings and then "dumping" them in anger.

10. Keep engendering hope and encouragement directly by saying things such as "You are working very hard on trying to control

your anger. It took a long time for you to get to this point, and it is going to take more time for you to master this, but you will, and we will help and encourage you."

Don't

1. Let the children sit back and stop working just because they have made some progress; keep challenging them to continue working and practicing new behaviors.

2. Let members leave group with heavy feelings in a raw state; if a child is very upset, stay with that child after the group leaves or go back to the classroom with the child to help him or her gain composure and process what happened.

3. Be surprised if reluctance and resistance resurface. Trust is not dealt with "once and for all" at the beginning of the group; as members interact, some are likely to redevelop issues of fear, self-protection, monopolizing, avoiding, and unwillingness to disclose further. Be patient and deal with these defenses each time they come up.

4. Let up on your efforts to reinforce any and all attempts as well as successes at behavior change; encourage children to praise and reinforce other group members for their work outside the group between sessions.

5. Lessen efforts to help group members process what happened each session so they leave with a clear idea of what they accomplished and what they need to work on during the next session.

Final Stage

Many group leaders do not recognize the importance of using the final stage of the group as a special learning experience that reaches beyond the bounds of the group sessions. This stage is unique and should be handled with utmost care. In our society we have a great deal of difficulty saying good-bye in relationships, whether it is at the death of a loved one, the end of a marriage, the loss of a pet, or a dear friend's departure. Many children are torn apart by the loss of a precious relative, pet, or friendship without the opportunity to say good-bye to the loved one or without knowing why or what has happened. Many teens have powerful romantic alliances that end in cruel ways, when the loved one suddenly decides to leave the relationship for someone else or for some reason that is not revealed to the partner.

Since most adults don't have the skills to deal with loss either, children often do not have positive role models for ending relationships. Ending a group experience provides an opportunity to teach this important skill. If you are uncomfortable dealing with loss or do not recognize what needs to be done at this time, the children can lose the chance to gain a significant skill for future relationships.

The therapeutic interaction skill "Closing Rituals" gives specific suggestions for using rituals as a way to close the group. Some general guidelines for this stage of the group follow.

Do

1. Ask the children to review their goals about three-quarters of the way through the group to determine how they are progressing and whether they need to do something different to meet their goals by the end of the group's sessions.

2. Make a conscious effort to inform children that the group experience is coming to a close two or three sessions before the last session.

3. Directly tell the children that they will be saying good-bye to one another and probably will never be together again exactly as they have been in the group. Indicate that they need to start thinking about how they want to let other members know they will be supporting their work and growth outside the group.

4. At the last session, help the children deal with their feelings about saying good-bye and separating from their support system. Encourage them to say whatever they need to say to other group members to finish unfinished feelings or issues.

5. Work with the children to make plans to continue working on their issues after the group finishes.

6. Be sure to let group members know that you will be available to help them if strong feelings or issues have been brought up as a result of the group but haven't been resolved.

7. Inform the children that you will be calling them together one more time as a group in a few weeks to review how they have been doing and provide support and encouragement.

8. Assist the children in developing and naming their own support system outside the group so they know whom to go to with problems related to the group's topic or focus.

9. At the last session, briefly go through the topics discussed at each of the previous sessions, asking children what they learned from that session, then ask them what they learned overall from the group.

10. Involve the children in creating whatever kind of closing experience they would like to have. Prepare some type of celebration activity to let the children know that their efforts are appreciated and that they can learn to appreciate one another's efforts.

Don't

1. Let the group sessions go by until the next-to-last or last session without reminding the children that the group will be ending.

2. Fail to plan how you are going to manage the last session, celebrate, deal with reviews or sad feelings, and so forth.

3. Let the group end in conflict or with a lot of unresolved negative feelings; deal with these beforehand.

4. End the group without having the members say good-bye and thank-you to one another.

5. Use the last session to conduct the posttest; have members stop by your office at a later time, give the posttest to them and have them return it to you, or administer it during the follow-up session.

6. Let children leave group without a support system if they need more help; make referrals to other groups or other types of counseling that might be available.

Using Problem Situations as Learning Experiences

This next section discusses situations that arise in group work that may be problematic for the leader and/or the members. These situations present unique opportunities for everyone to learn something about interpersonal relationships, how they work, and how to improve them. These problems parallel those in group work with adults. However, children usually have less social control than adults do and therefore act out more readily. Sometimes children who have difficulty in group are viewed as "problem members." It is more helpful for everyone involved if you take the view that problems in the group are learning opportunities in disguise.

Some of the most problematic behaviors that arise in group work with younger children include anger, monopolizing, attention seeking (showing-off behaviors), resistance, and shyness. Some of the most problematic situations encountered in group work with older youths are breaking confidentiality, cliques within the group, arguments and fighting, and contagious exiting. A final issue, crying, arises with children of all ages, depending on the topic and the trust level of the group.

Anger

Many children come to the group experience with a great deal of anger inside. Sometimes the anger is not even inside but very close to the surface. Anger has many faces and is dealt with in numerous ways. You are likely to have children who *act out* their anger by making nasty comments, cursing, threatening to hit another group member, talking back to the leader, and so forth. Some children *act in* their anger, repressing it to the point where they somatize it and become ill or develop other psychological symptoms. Some use their angry energy to motivate them to succeed at schoolwork or athletics.

How can you deal with an angry child? This depends on whether (a) the child enters the group with a great deal of anger and the anger is being brought out in the group or (b) the child becomes angry at something that happens related to the group experience, either in a session or between sessions.

You can find out during the screening process whether a child who is full of anger from his or her life experiences is an appropriate candidate for group in the first place. You have the responsibility to question whether a child with a history of acting out will be a source of conflict and possible harm to the other group members. If during the selection process you determine that a child acts out his or her anger in inappropriate ways, then you will need to think about the consequences, because this behavior is going to happen in group. The group is a microcosm of the child's milieu, and the situations that precipitate the child's angry aggression will eventually occur. Will you be able to handle this child's anger so it does not take away from the other group members' rights to be safe and have equal time? Unless the group is involuntary and/or you are experienced in dealing with severely resistant and aggressive behaviors, it is best not to include this child.

This advice does not necessarily exclude the many children who have a great deal of anger from their life situations, such as stress involved in dealing with parental divorce conflict, parental alcoholism or substance abuse, physical and/or sexual abuse, and so on. Children with a great deal of anger can be in a group—many are, with excellent success in learning to understand and manage their anger. How can you deal with acting-out anger in the group?

First, you must be able to assure other children that you understand their fears of being threatened physically by the aggressive member. Try to determine whether the threat of aggression is coming from the member's behavior or from your own aggressive feelings, which are stirred up by the member's behavior. When you are experiencing fear of aggression in the group, you may be tempted to suppress the expression of anger. This may result in that anger's indirect expression—for example, through offensive language or passive-aggressive behavior. If your fear is coming from within, it is important to remember that aggressive verbalizations do not necessarily denote that violence will ensue. If fear of aggression in the group is coming from quickly escalating negative interactions among members, you will need to intervene by offering to use the situation as a learning experience to explore what the differences are about and what can be done to resolve them.

Second, if the anger and potential aggression are coming from a particular member, you can use physical activities in the session to help teach appropriate ways to externalize that anger—for example, hitting a punching bag, throwing balls in a wastebasket, drawing pictures or making sculptures to express the anger, or engaging in other play therapy. Because externalizing activities give children the opportunity to release their feelings, they can be especially helpful to children who act in their anger.

Be accepting of anger, giving each child in the group the opportunity to express this emotion. Use go-arounds, such as "Today I feel most angry about . . ." so all of the children in the group realize that anger is a natural human emotion. Don't suppress the natural expression of anger. Reinforce it and allow the children to have their feelings, even if it makes you uncomfortable. Remember, most of us had parents who did not allow us to feel our feelings. As a result, we have had a difficult time learning to express them.

Third, adjust your expectations of children to be realistic. Try to understand that young people's world is very different from our own—they have so many adults in their lives trying to control them, and many come to group skeptical, doubtful, and resistant that any adults are "on their side." Sometimes you might need to work with group members just to come to group and listen, rather than pressing them to share and work and change. Some children are angry through and through. These children need patience and love and consistency to get to the point where they are ready to work. Be a model for them by accepting them, even their angry, hostile feelings and behaviors, and help them to see the reason for their behaviors is that they are afraid and hurt. Encourage them to understand that it is OK for them to be angry, but that they must find new ways to express their anger—it isn't OK to hurt others just because you are hurting.

If a child's anger is provoked by something that happens in the group, rather than in that child's life outside the group, you can use the situation as grist for the mill. Invite the member or members who are angry to explore their negative feelings and find out what is happening to provoke the anger. Perhaps a member has different ideas, values, or preferences and is pressuring another member to accept his or her ideas. Or a member may belittle, scapegoat, or ridicule another member, who then becomes very angry. You can say, "What is it about what Marcus is saying that makes you mad?" and "Tell Marcus how you feel when he makes fun of you." Ask other members to become involved and think about how they might feel in this situation and let them share. Many children come from families where anger is not OK or anger is expressed inappropriately and have never seen anger dealt with appropriately. Get the anger and hurt out in the open and let children see you model positive ways of dealing with these emotions.

Monopolizing

Children monopolize the "air time" in group for different reasons and in different ways. Some self-disclose too often and only on superficial issues, adding little to the sharing. Some self-disclose in such depth that it frightens shyer and lower self-disclosing children because they think that this is what is expected of them also. Other monopolizers interrupt frequently by adding that the same situation happened to them, thus taking away from the child who is sharing and redirecting the group's attention toward themselves.

The underlying reasons children monopolize are usually fear and anxiety. Since most monopolizers are not saying anything substantial, they manage to appear to be working group members but are actually using this as a way to keep from having to work, change, or learn new skills. Such children are usually afraid to deal with their problems, afraid to admit that they need to change, and/or afraid that they will be ridiculed by their peers. Young adolescents, especially, are afraid their friends will not think they are "cool" if they want to improve, and their motivation for change might be shaky at best. Some children who ramble on and on are unaware that their repetition of situations or long, drawn-out stories are boring to other members. This kind of monopolizing is easy to spot and needs to be stopped because the other children also spot it quickly. They will get angry if you allow the member to take up all of the group time.

Monopolizing is a way for younger children to get some badly needed attention. There may be no one in their young lives who gives them any positive attention, listens to them, or accepts them in a nonjudgmental way. To be in a situation where they can command the attention of a significant adult and other children is overpowering.

Ethically, you have the responsibility to ensure equitable use of time for all members. It is up to you to protect this. If monopolizing goes on long enough and you do not intervene, the group members will become aggravated and eventually confront the monopolizer. But by this time the irritation may have caused some of the group members to "turn off" to the group experience. You can prevent this by dealing with monopolizing early on. However, being confronted by peers may be just what some youths need to help them understand how they are coming across—better than anything any adult could say!

Here are some specific techniques to deal with the situation when a child monopolizes:

1. Try to assess how long the child has been talking in comparison to the other group members. Make a judgment about whether the monopolizing child is keeping others from talking and if others are becoming bored and/or irritated. If so, it is time to

intervene directly. You might need to say, "Latisha, you have had a lot of air time today. Please let everyone else have a chance to talk before it's your turn again." Or, addressing the problem more directly, you could say, "Taylor, you seem to need a lot of attention today. What seems to be bothering you that needs to come out?"

2. Help the child to explore and learn why he or she is engaging in this behavior—whether it is out of anxiety, avoidance, trying to control the group, or getting attention from you and/or other members. Invite the child to take a look at some of the reasons for the behavior and how it is affecting the rest of the group.

3. Corey and Corey (1992) suggest that you ask the group member to respond to sentence stems such as "If I didn't talk . . ."; "I have a lot to say because . . ."; and "I want you to listen to me because . . . ." These may be used with adolescents; however, younger children will usually shut down if quizzed in this way.

4. Help the children learn to discriminate between telling long stories about their life or peripheral people and talking about themselves and immediate issues. Many children just don't know what you mean by talking about themselves versus talking about the many people in their lives. They are not used to being asked how they feel, what they think, how their behavior is affecting others, or what they want to learn.

Attention Seeking

The attention seeker or show-off is engaging in manipulative behavior for the purpose of getting his or her own needs met at the expense of other group members. Attention-seeking children desperately need to be affirmed, accepted, and acknowledged, but they are going about getting their emotional "fix" in negative ways, which they have no doubt learned long before the group experience. They have probably been engaging in these kinds of behaviors for many years and in a variety of ways that they have found work for them. These children are frequently insecure and want to impress others with what they know, have done, or are going to do.

To help you confront this problem, be sure to reinforce the child for appropriate behaviors and self-disclosures in the group, with the understanding that he or she needs attention badly.

Avoid positive nonverbal behaviors such as smiling, agreeing, nodding, and praising the child when he or she is engaging in negative, attention-seeking behaviors.

You could also ask the group members to form dyads, pairing yourself with the show-off. While together, you can discuss the behavior with the attention seeker without causing embarrassment in front of the whole group, privately attempting to find out the child's needs and stressing the need for sharing group time. This approach can work; however, the show-off behavior may escalate if the child is very hostile and needs to control the group or is revengeful toward you. At that point it would be better to bring the issue up to the whole group and let them talk about how the show-off behavior affects each one of them.

A direct approach is sometimes best: You cut off the member who is going on and on by saying, for example, "Juan, I need to stop you here because others need time to talk also." If you do, be sure to follow the suggestions given for the leadership skill "Cutting Off."

Resistance

It sometimes seems that resistant group members are deliberately trying to anger us, but this is not usually the case. On the contrary, resistance is usually self-protective rather than a deliberate attempt to anger and frustrate the counselor.

Some classic research with juvenile delinquents conducted by Gadpaille (1959) identified three phases of group resistance: open defiance, testing, and group silence. In the first phase, Gadpaille experienced group members directly defying the leader, expressing mistrust, offering to cause harm, walking out of sessions, and insisting that the leader wasn't a "doctor." In the second phase, testing, youths attempted to provoke the leader to anger to determine whether his response would be the same as other adults'. This stage did not begin until the group members realized that the leader was not going to be bullied into quitting the group in spite of their behavior of the previous stage. The youths wanted to know if the leader could be trusted and did so by bragging about delinquent acts, using obscene language, and attacking other adults verbally. The third phase of resistance was silence, which occurred when the group perceived that the leader had let them down or rejected them in some way.

Although these were the openly hostile expressions of delinquent youths, they have their parallels in more average-functioning youths.

74

These three types of resistant behaviors are the source of conflict and keep group members from dealing with their own issues. They are frequently attempts to keep the focus off painful feelings by focusing on external events and behaviors.

To help group members work through resistance, remember that most resistance is usually justified caution coming from youths who have reasons to be cautious about self-disclosing to adults and other peers. Generally, it is not a deliberate attack on you as the leader.

If you are dealing with a population likely to present a great deal of resistant behavior, it would be a good idea to meet with each group member individually before the group starts. Spend as much time as possible letting members know the group is there to help them explore their goals; encourage them to vent their anger and frustrations about being required to be in the group. If the group is involuntary, tell prospective members that even though they do not have a choice about being there, they have all the same rights as voluntary group members, except the right not to attend. They can choose not to participate if they like. The group experience has an emotional appeal, and they will usually begin participating to some extent before long. By having some freedom in choosing their level of participation, they feel a little more in control and less in need of controlling. In most cases, working with resistance is more helpful than working against it. You don't fight fire with fire—you fight fire with water.

If you have just one or two resistant members rather than a whole group of resistant youths, don't focus on the resistant ones, trying to break down their resistance. Let them have the opportunity to vent their anger about having to be in the group. After this, let them be and give the group process a chance to work.

If a member is hostile, silent, or sarcastic, acknowledge that individual's feelings and invite the person to share what it is like to feel hostile or be silent or sarcastic. For example, you could say, "Carmen, you sound very angry about being here, and perhaps you don't want to come to group. That must be an awful feeling for you. What is it like for you to be angry about being here?"

If the resistant member is resistant only toward you and not toward other members, have the group work together in dyads or on projects to get the member involved and past the need to be resistant. Use action-oriented techniques and activities that appeal to youths. Don't expect them to sit there and do talk therapy like adults! Get them doing something active or creative, learning skills through practice, and so on.

Shyness

The shy child presents an interesting dilemma. It is difficult to find information in counseling books about shy children and how to help them because shyness is most commonly viewed as a lack of social skills. Since shy children appear to have underdeveloped social skills, some think that all it takes is teaching them the skills and the shyness will go away. To a certain extent this is true, but it is also important to consider the origin of the shyness.

A child might be shy for many reasons, including poor role models at home, lack of exposure to a variety of people and situations during early childhood, physiological temperament, social isolation as a very young child, strongly negative experiences in early childhood (e.g., physical or sexual abuse), abuse or control by siblings and/or peers, developmental disabilities, or physical disabilities that prohibit frequent, sustained positive relationships. For any of these or other reasons, the shy child feels more comfortable being an observer than risking participation in social situations.

In a small group, there are fewer children and more time and energy focused on each one. This can be very anxiety producing for the shy child. Couple this with a leader who is anxious to follow the ethical guidelines and provide equal time for group members, and you have a situation where the child can become quite fearful indeed.

Here are some techniques you can use to help the shy child participate:

1. Try to empathize with the shy child. In the small-group situation, it is not as easy to be an unnoticed wallflower as in the classroom.

2. Be sure to role balance during the selection procedure so you have models for the shy child to learn effective ways of communicating. For example, include two shy children along with children who have average and above average social skills. Avoid having just one shy child, or he or she will feel all alone and won't experience a sense of universality as easily.

3. Plan activities so that you can pair the shy child with a child who has very good social skills; this will help the shy child learn from modeling.

4. Give gentle encouragement to participate. Say things such as "There are some we haven't heard from today. Let's let them share if they'd like"; "Maria, what do you think about what we've been talking about?"; "Aziza, who has said something in group that you connect with?"

5. Do not prod. If you do, you will get a "safe" resistant response or a refusal (e.g., "I don't know").

6. Don't remind the member of a promise to be an active group member. If you do, he or she will be more insecure and silent.

7. Watch to see how the other group members deal with the shy member. Try to have other members connect with regard to the shy member's feelings, attitudes, and beliefs.

There is evidence to suggest that group members can remain silent and still profit from the learning of others, so allow the withdrawn member some time to figure out the group process. Some children need more time to adjust to new and threatening situations. Allow the group process to take place. Many children have trouble developing trusting relationships with adults and eventually learn more from their peers than from adults. Give the shy child space and time.

Breaking Confidentiality

Breeches of confidentiality are serious business in group work because the basis for self-disclosure in groups is trust, including trust that other group members will keep disclosures confidential. Without trust, there is no disclosure. Without disclosure, there is no group work. Children and adolescents with trust issues have a pervasive mistrust of adults and other children who have information about them that puts them in a vulnerable position. They may see the group as a very scary place to be.

It can take a great deal of your time, energy, and skill to prepare for and begin the group with the utmost attention to the trust issue. You will need to discuss the issue of confidentiality with prospective group members, including what you are doing to assure that all group members are aware of the importance of confidentiality and the consequences of breaking this trust. As discussed previously, this will involve clarifying the limits of confidentiality. Despite your efforts, you cannot ensure that confidentiality will remain unbroken, and the children are well aware of this fact.

Corey and Corey (1992) point out that group members need to be instructed that they could break confidentiality outside the group nonmaliciously, through carelessness. Sometimes young children just don't realize what confidentiality means. Discussing examples like the following will help:

> Jason and Kareem are in a group at their school to work on changing behaviors that get them in trouble. They live on the same street with Jason's best friend, Jackie, and Kareem's best friend, D.J. The four of them are outside hanging out one evening when Jason adds several curse words to a statement he has just made. Then Kareem says, "Oh, Jason, you aren't supposed to say words like that—remember what you promised in group." Was Kareem breaking confidentiality?

> Melanie and Melissa are twins. Melissa is in a group at the mental health center to help her be less shy and learn social skills. Melanie decided she did not want to be in a group, even though her mom and teachers thought she would be helped by the group experience. Melissa came home from group today and told Melanie that she learned how to make new friends by introducing herself to other kids at school. Was Melissa breaking confidentiality?

Be sure to have the children participate in determining the consequences for breaking confidentiality. This helps to demystify the concept and gives them a sense of ownership that they need to be active in the process. If there is an outside agency involved, such as juvenile court, be sure to let the group members know what is being expected of you in terms of reporting progress in counseling to the probation officer or judge. Whatever is decided, make sure it is clear and simple and that every group member can repeat what the consequences are for breaking confidentiality.

If a breach of confidentiality occurs, encourage the children to vent their anger, disappointment, and hurt. Give everyone a chance to say how he or she feels about the situation. The children need to know that you respect their feelings and the feelings of other members and that you will uphold the stated plan for dealing with a breech in confidentiality. Remember that emphasizing confidentiality is a type of limit setting, and some adolescents are just waiting for you to set limits so they can rebel and exceed them. They are testing you to see if you will remain steadfast to what you have said and if you really care enough about them to follow through.

When a group member says another group member has disclosed confidential information, take sufficient time to deal with the situation. Nothing else is as important as using this event as a learning experience. Let the person share what he or she heard. Invite the child who is supposed to have disclosed to share his or her side of the story. Then allow each of the children in the group to have a say in what they think about the situation and what should be done. You can rarely go wrong in letting the group deal with this themselves, as they are usually the best judge and jury of their peers. Rarely have I ever felt uncomfortable about the outcome of a situation when I let them hash it out among themselves, serving as coordinator, facilitator, and, when necessary, protector.

Cliques

A clique is a small subgroup or pair who come into the group already having a special connection or who develop connections within the group. As noted earlier, it is important to avoid selecting members for the group who have existing special relationships, either positive or negative (i.e., best friends or worst enemies). However, it is not always possible to know whether certain individuals are part of a larger "in-group" in the school or institution.

Cliques are exclusionary by nature and can be harmful to the development of cohesion and trust in the group. They can also be opportunities for learning for all of the members, as their resolution usually provides a deeper sense of cohesion than existed before.

Once the group begins, cliques develop among members who perceive one another to be of high status. The forming of cliques, also known as "flocking" (Levine, 1991), usually happens during the beginning group stages. Seeking to be identified with other valuable members, members begin linking behaviors in the group. It is extremely important to children, especially as they reach middle school age and older, to be accepted by those in their social role and status groups. So it is natural when a new group is formed artificially, as is the case with the group counseling experience, that jockeying for position takes place immediately. Another reason cliques form is that it is simply more comfortable psychologically to relate to one, two, or three others than to seven or eight others.

Cliques develop among youths who have a high social hunger and a strong need to be identified with other youths who have attained whatever success is deemed important. For example, if a child needs to be recognized as a "jock," that child will dress, act, talk, and behave in ways that the "jock" group recognizes and rewards and try to be included among the "jocks." Another child might want to be identified with those considered most fashionable—whatever that happens to be—and go to great trouble to have the right clothes, hairstyle, and so forth to fit in with that clique.

Sometimes conflicts develop between the "in group" and the "out group," or those in the clique and those who are not in the clique. It is by working through the conflicts of the clique and out-group that a real sense of cohesion can develop. In a conflict situation, you can develop the sense of common beliefs and emotions that will begin to break down the barriers. It is important to use the clique to help break down the barriers rather than to try to squelch it, pretend it doesn't exist, or create further hostility in group members, who already have plenty of anger, fear, anxiety, and pain.

Along with a clique in a group you also may have individuals who have unresolved issues about trust and little sense of universality or cohesion. They may be trying to resist clique pressure by forming one-on-one relationships or alliances with you in lieu of getting involved with the existing clique or forming another clique or subgroup. It is also important to be aware that aversions between group members occur. Such aversions are generally based on age, socioeconomic status, status within the peer culture, or other real or perceived differences.

A short-term group is very prone to cliques, especially at the high-risk age levels (middle school and older). Unfortunately, many short-term groups are so short that the clique phenomenon cannot be explored appropriately and used as a vehicle to grow. In the group, you will need to use techniques to foster the equal use of time and group energy and not permit certain members to take over. Here are some techniques you can use to encourage equal participation and diminish clique behavior.

1. When you realize that certain members are colluding to the exclusion of other members, try to put some distance between them, especially if they are inclined to "horse around" with one another. Reassign seats so that the clique members are not seated

next to each other. This is a start and can work in the beginning to keep cliques from solidifying.

2. Pair members in working dyads so that you have one clique member and one non-clique member working together. Part of the reason some children are excluded is that they are unknown to others, and working in dyads gives children the opportunity to get to know one another. Assign a task or activity that takes some interaction, perhaps outside of group, such as looking up information or gathering materials for making a collage. This helps them get in touch as people and can encourage them to value their differences.

3. If the issue of perceived or actual differences starts to get in the way of the group members' working on their problems, bring this out into the open and make it a group issue. You could say, for example, "I've been noticing that several of you seem to be tuning out some of the other members of the group. Let's talk about what that means to all of us."

Arguments and Fighting

Arguments are a natural occurrence in groups because differences of opinion come up regularly in any interpersonal relationship. However, children frequently don't have the verbal skills to deal with disagreements nor the conflict resolution skills to help themselves. In group, arguments present a splendid opportunity. First, they can be used as the springboard to teach conflict resolution skills as effective and appropriate ways to deal with anger and disagreements. Second, arguments allow heavy emotions to bubble out, which are energy for deeper connections among the children. You can use these emotions to help children get connected, identify with one side of the argument or the other, or explore their own views on the subject. Third, arguments are opportunities to teach tolerance and appreciation of diversity in values, ideas, attitudes, and beliefs.

If an argument escalates into a physical fight or some other form of destruction, such as throwing chairs or other objects, it must be stopped immediately for the safety of all group members. Most groups have a "no fighting" ground rule, and this should be enforced immediately. All group members are at risk of being hurt in a physical fight, not just the combatants. Highly aggressive adolescents (e.g., delinquents, youths on probation or in inpatient settings) are particularly vulnerable to this behavior. In such high-risk groups, clear consequences for fighting need to be stated at the beginning. Some youths deliberately begin fights to be ejected from the group (a secondary gain), so be certain that this consequence is not actually reinforcing.

Use differences of opinion as a learning experiment. When you notice that two or more group members appear to be lining up on different sides of an issue or have very different thoughts about something, invite them to bring their differences out in the open, then encourage the rest of the group to choose one of the two different opinions, or another one altogether.

Consider the following example: Karen and Annie are in a group for children of divorce. Annie's parents have both remarried, and she has a stepsister and two stepbrothers. Karen's parents have not remarried, but her mother is dating a man whom Karen dislikes. Karen is very angry at her mother and in the group. She strongly states that she believes that parents should not get married again until the kids have grown up so the kids don't have to put up with losing their mom's time, having a stepdad tell you what to do all the time, and having to share space with stepbrothers and stepsisters. Annie has a very different opinion because she has adjusted to her new stepfamily and likes having someone to play with and with whom to share toys and clothes. Karen and Annie get red in the face and begin an argument about which is better, for parents to remarry or to stay unmarried until the kids grow up. The leader picks up on Annie's and Karen's anger and hurt in the group and says, "It sounds to me like Karen and Annie have very different ideas about what parents ought to do about remarriage after a divorce. I'm wondering if the rest of you agree with Annie, or agree with Karen, or have some other opinion about this situation. What do you think? Would you be willing to share that with us? . . . Well, then, let's make a list of the different ideas about this situation." After the opinions are shared, the group discusses the positive and negative aspects of each. The leader then asks about having different opinions, using the following types of process questions:

> What do you think now about what divorced persons
> ought to do? What did you find out about having different
> opinions or beliefs about this?

What is a good way to handle disagreements between two or more people?

What did you like about letting everyone share an opinion?

What is good about being open and accepting about other people's opinions?

What happens when you share different opinions without trying to change or hurt the other person?

What have you learned about problem solving?

If a fight erupts in the group—hitting, throwing things, or threatening—you can say "time-out" in a loud voice, repeating this if necessary. If the conflict and hostility are so great that it would disrupt the group for the fighting members to remain, dismiss them one at a time, possibly with another group member to escort them back to their class or room. If you need assistance, call another adult to help break the fight up and protect others from getting hurt. Let the fighting group members know they will have an opportunity to meet with you later to defuse the situation. If you think it would be productive for the whole group to process what happened, then do so. If the fighting members have left the room, take some time to process what happened and move on as necessary. This kind of situation leaves group members wondering whether they are safe or if they too will be ejected if they disagree. You will need to assure them that disagreements are welcome but that inappropriate ways of dealing with them are not.

A group of young adolescents, from about 12 to 15 years old, is difficult to work with but has powerful therapeutic potential. Remember that their peer group is the most important aspect of their lives and that they have significant difficulty with impulse control regarding their friendships, emerging sexuality, academic life, and relationships with adults. Fighting and aggression are common because many have not learned to handle misunderstandings in any other way than fighting. Thompson and Rudolph (1992) suggest being an "environmental engineer" to help youths avoid situations likely to produce fighting. In a group, you can do this by managing seating arrangements, listening carefully for escalating tone of voice, watching for signs of anger, and trying to defuse group members' anger before it erupts.

In addition to controlling the environment, you will need to assess the motivation of the fighters. Are the combatants seeking power and control in the group, revenge on another member, or attention from you and/or other members? Other reasons for fighting might be lack of other behavioral skills to deal with negative emotions, learned helplessness, and poor role models for appropriate anger management. Depending on the goals of the misbehavior, you can design ways to help the fighters learn alternatives to aggression.

You might need to revisit the ground rules with the group. If clear guidelines concerning fighting were not established in the beginning of the group, after a fight is certainly a time to do so. Have all of the members participate in telling how they feel about being hit or hurt, what it is like to feel unsafe, and what they need to feel safe. Clearly state consequences for fighting and be sure everyone understands. When you judge that a fight might occur, you can refer to the ground rule for fighting, saying, "What is our ground rule about fighting—what happens if there is a fight? Let's talk about what is happening right now to make you so mad you want to fight."

If the group is high risk and/or fights break out frequently, you might need to have group members sign a behavioral contract for not fighting. If there is no fighting in the group for that session, have a reward for everyone. If the contract is a private one between you and a particular group member, reward according to the contract. (Specific suggestions for developing and using contracts are presented in the discussion of the therapeutic interaction technique "Contracting.")

Skills-based approaches can also help reduce aggression. In group, brainstorm alternatives to fighting. Have group members prioritize new skills, then teach them. Many good resources for skills-based learning exist (e.g., Goldstein, Sprafkin, Gershaw, & Klein, 1980; McGinnis & Goldstein, 1984). Stress management skills like the "Progressive Muscle Relaxation" therapeutic interaction skill and stress inoculation methods (Meichenbaum, 1985) are other alternatives to aggression. Stories, videotapes, or films also can be good stimuli for discussion about fighting and its consequences.

Finally, you can use positive peer pressure to help fighters reduce their aggressiveness toward each other. Pair fighters with peers who have good self-control and know how to manage stressful situations. Lectures from adults generally fall on deaf ears, whereas messages from peers come through loud and clear.

Contagious Exiting

Contagious exiting occurs when one child decides for whatever reason to leave the group, and suddenly one or more other children decide to leave also. Unless the group is involuntary, the children have a right to leave. What can you do to keep the whole group from dissolving?

The first step in dealing with this situation is prevention. Once you have told group members about and feel they understand their right to leave, do not repeat this information every session as you would the confidentiality rule. Members may be anxious and insecure at the beginning of a group and as yet have little experience of the cohesion, universality, trust, or other strong therapeutic forces that will eventually encourage continued membership. If you keep repeating that members have a right to leave, some will invariably take you up on the invitation. In the beginning, it may be easier to quit than to stick it out.

It is also a good idea to set guidelines for leaving the group once it starts. Having a group member leave, even after a few sessions, disrupts the emotional equilibrium of the group. The person is missed in proportion to how much he or she added to or hurt the group. Even a member who was an aggravation to the others leaves behind a pervasive sense of relief that occupies the group for a session or two. The change requires group energy. I recommend telling prospective group members that if they choose to leave, it will affect everyone else in the group so they will need to come to one last session to share their intention to leave and say good-bye. They don't have to give their reasons, although they could, but they do need to give the group a chance to say good-bye. This gives the group the opportunity to explore what is scary about being in the group. Sometimes a member who intends to leave derives enough support and relief from bringing this fear out into the open that he or she decides to stay in the group.

Most children do not know what it means to learn new skills and behaviors and work on changing themselves. This is an unknown experience and is therefore anxiety producing. Many do not want to change or do not understand why they should change, other than that their teachers or parents don't appreciate their behavior. When they realize after a session or two that there are expectations for change and see other children learning new skills, the internal pressure to exit builds up. When one child leaves, for whatever reason, other children who might be high in anxiety and low in commitment might begin to think about leaving also. When a second member decides to leave, it is time to bring a discussion of the fears, worries, and concerns the members have out into the open. By doing so you may discover something going on that you didn't realize—maybe the fears of certain group members are more intense than you knew or unfounded fears and worries may exist. An open discussion of the fact that it is hard, scary, and takes a lot of courage to change may be what is needed to bring emotional relief. After this discussion, it is a good idea to revisit individual goals, with an assessment of how group members are doing. For example, you could say:

> We've been talking about how hard it is to change and
> learn new ways of doing things when we have been
> doing them a certain way for some time. What about
> your goals for the group? Are they real goals for you,
> or maybe they need to be changed a little to make them
> easier for you to reach and not be discouraging. What do
> you think?

Crying

Crying is a natural physiological process our body uses to relieve psychological pain. Children are more emotionally vulnerable than adults and have less social control. They are therefore more likely to cry during a group experience. The older they are, however, the more control they gain. By high school, unfortunately, they are able to choke back a significant amount of emotional pain. Some youths are very controlled and wouldn't let their peers see them cry for anything. In any group you will have a range of ability to express psychological pain through tears. Some children might just tear up, and others might cry quite uncontrollably for several minutes.

Although older children and adolescents are less likely to cry, crying in group is related more to the group topic and stage of group development than to the age of the members. Some groups for youths deal with topics that are more likely to provide opportunities for crying than others. For example, a group on loss issues is very likely to provoke tears. Other issues that are particularly sensitive are single parenthood for teens, relationship breakups, and parental divorce. The further along a group is in its life process and the greater the level of trust, the more likely participants are to feel comfortable letting their tears flow.

Since tears are our natural way of letting out psychological pain, you will need to know how to handle this situation to make it a helpful experience for everyone. Here are some suggestions and techniques for dealing with tears.

1. Try to determine whether the child is crying out of genuine psychological pain or trying to get sympathy. Occasionally, the child might be doing and saying things that bring attention, hugs, and sympathetic statements from others. Sometimes this is not easy to determine, but if crying is frequent and you begin to get the feeling that a "poor me" game is going on, then it would not be beneficial to reinforce this kind of behavior (Jacobs, Harvill, & Masson, 1994).

2. Most of the time, crying is truly an expression of pain. When a child starts to cry, ask the child if he or she wants to talk about and share the painful feelings rather than assuming that the child does. Sometimes the child does not feel comfortable sharing in the group and will need to be allowed to deal with the pain on his or her own timetable. Tears can be quite spontaneous, and the child might not be ready to talk.

3. If the child is sobbing deeply about something that he or she has shared, the leader might want to let the child cry for a period of time and then initiate a discussion with the other members about what it must be like to feel such fear, anger, loss, whatever. When the child indicates a willingness to talk, let him or her have center stage.

4. Another caution given by Jacobs et al. (1994) is to take note of the time left in the session. If the child is crying at the end of the session, you might want to say, for example, "Tina, I know this must hurt you a lot. Let's talk more about this after the group is over." By letting other group members know that the child will not have to go back to class or leave for home without having time to process feelings, you assure them that they will have time in the session to deal with their own feelings. This respects everyone's needs.

5. Always bring tissues to group! Set a box in the center of the circle at the beginning of the session so everyone gets the message that group is a place where it is safe and appropriate to cry if you need to.

In addition to the problematic behaviors and situations just described, other sticky situations will also occur and challenge you to learn new ways of handling many young clients at once. You can rely on your ethical guidelines and the clinical judgment of experienced practitioners to help you deal with these group work opportunities.

Resources

Allen, F. H. (1979). Therapeutic work with children. In C. Schaefer (Ed.), *The therapeutic use of child's play* (pp. 227–238). New York: Jason Aronson.

Association for Specialists in Group Work. (1989). *Professional standards for the training of group workers.* (Available from ASGW/ACA, 5999 Stevenson Avenue, Alexandria, Virginia 22304.)

Association for Specialists in Group Work. (1990). Ethical guidelines for group counselors. *Journal for Specialists in Group Work, 15*(2), 119–126.

Axline, V. (1947). *Play therapy.* Boston: Houghton Mifflin.

Bruckner, S., & Thompson, C. (1987). Guidance program evaluation: An example. *Elementary School Guidance and Counseling, 21,* 193–196.

Corey, M. S., & Corey, G. (1992). *Groups: Process and practice* (4th ed.). Pacific Grove: Brooks/Cole.

Corey, G., Corey, M. S., Callanan, P., & Russell, J. M. (1992). *Group techniques* (2nd ed.). Pacific Grove, CA: Brooks/Cole.

Cormier, W. H., & Cormier, L. S. (1991). *Interviewing strategies for helpers* (3rd ed.). Pacific Grove, CA: Brooks/Cole.

Ehly, S., & Dustin, D. (1991). *Individual and group counseling in the schools.* New York: Guilford.

Gadpaille, W. J. (1959). Observations on the sequence of resistances in groups of adolescent delinquents. *International Journal of Group Psychotherapy, 9,* 275–286.

Gardner, D. (1983). *A nation at risk: The imperative for educational reform.* Washington, DC: U.S. Department of Education.

Gazda, G. M. (1989). *Group counseling: A developmental approach* (chap. 13). Boston: Allyn & Bacon.

Goldstein, A. P., Sprafkin, R. P., Gershaw, N. J., & Klein, P. (1980). *Skillstreaming the adolescent: A structured learning approach to teaching prosocial skills.* Champaign, IL: Research Press.

Jacobs, E. E., Harvill, R. L., & Masson, R. L. (1994). *Group counseling: Strategies and skills* (2nd ed.). Pacific Grove, CA: Brooks/Cole.

Levine, B. (1991). *Group psychotherapy: Practice and development.* Prospect Heights, IL: Waveland.

McGinnis, E., & Goldstein, A. P. (1984). *Skillstreaming the elementary school child: A guide for teaching prosocial skills.* Champaign, IL: Research Press.

Meichenbaum, D. H. (1985). *Stress inoculation training.* New York: Pergamon.

Morganett, R. S. (1990). *Skills for living: Group counseling activities for young adolescents.* Champaign, IL: Research Press.

Morganett, R. S. (1994). *Skills for living: Group counseling activities for elementary students.* Champaign, IL: Research Press.

O'Connor, K. J. (1991). *The play therapy primer: An integration of theories and techniques.* New York: Wiley.

Stone, L., & Bradley, F. (1994). *Foundations of elementary and middle school counseling.* White Plains, NY: Longman.

Thompson, C. L., & Rudolph, L. (1992). *Counseling children* (3rd ed.). Pacific Grove, CA: Brooks/Cole.

Tuckman, B. W. (1965). Developmental sequences in small groups. *Psychological Bulletin, 63,* 384–399.

Tuckman, B. W., & Jensen, M. A. (1977). Stages of small group development revisited. *Group and Organization, 2,* 419–427.

Witmer, J. M., & Young, M. E. (1987). Imagery in counseling. *Elementary School Guidance and Counseling, 22,* 5–16.

LEADERSHIP SKILLS

Ground Rules and Other Norms

Overview

Norms are the behaviors expected of group members—the rules, both explicit and implicit, that govern member conduct. Explicit norms, also known as *ground rules*, are expectations for behavior that are stated openly in the group. Ground rules concern such matters as coming to group on time, giving everyone a chance to talk, and maintaining confidentiality. Implicit norms are expectations for group behavior that facilitate the personal growth of each member and the development of the therapeutic dynamics of trust, cohesion, universality, and hope. Some examples of this type are speaking to one another instead of to the group leader, sharing and self-disclosing, and taking turns.

Rationale

The purpose of developing and reinforcing norms in the group is basically to let members know what behaviors are expected of them in this new setting and, ultimately, to facilitate the group's movement toward its stated goals. Norms give comfort, direction, and feedback to everyone about what is going on, what to continue doing, and what to change.

How to Use the Skill

In group work with children, it is extremely important to attend to the development of norms and to reinforce expected behaviors, especially during the first few sessions. Unless children have had some nontraditional classroom experiences or other group counseling experiences, they simply don't know how to behave in a group setting. They are used to classroom rules such as raising a hand to be recognized, established during elementary school. They need to know that group counseling has its own set of expected behaviors and that they will not be punished for not knowing what to do but rather will be guided to behave in a different way. All ground rules need to be adjusted according to the age and vocabulary of the children involved.

Ground Rules

Some ground rules are best discussed at the selection interview so the potential group member understands that certain rules will be followed and that these rules will provide some protection for the member. For example:

No alcohol or drugs just before or during group.

Participation is voluntary; any member may exit at any time.

You may say "I pass" and not take part in any activity or exercise.

You will be protected against physical threats, intimidation, coercion, and undue peer pressure.

One ground rule that is important to establish at the selection interview, as well as to stress over the life of the group, concerns confidentiality. To explain this issue, you might say something like the following:

Whatever we say in group stays in group. No one is allowed to share what anyone else says in group. There are certain times when I would have to share what you say—if you say something about harming yourself or others, if you share something about child abuse, or if the court (a judge) asks me what goes on.

The ethical guidelines of the Association for Specialists in Group Work (ASGW), reproduced in Appendix A of this book, will be helpful in establishing other ground rules for the group experience.

Insofar as possible, group members should be allowed to have the chance to help develop ground rules for their group. Doing so encourages them to have a sense of "ownership": If they are involved in making the rules, they are more likely to be invested in following them. Group members' input should be solicited during the first session.

Implicit Norms

Children are usually eager to know and quick to learn what is expected of them, and you can develop norms early on in the group that will set a positive tone for the sessions to follow. For example, you can reinforce doing self-improvement homework and participating in group activities or prevent one member from monopolizing the group's time. You might encourage the implicit norm of empathy among group members by modeling the use of empathic statements in support of group members' feelings and providing praise when group members make such statements. Similarly, you can support the norm that it is OK for each member to move at his or her own pace by showing acceptance of a range of self-disclosing behavior. Using a "turn teddy" or some other item, such as a stuffed pillow in the shape of a heart, can help you establish the norm of turn taking: A member must be in possession of the "turn teddy" to talk and when finished talking should pass it to someone else who wants to talk.

It is also possible for negative norms to develop in the group. For example, if you permit a member to make comments under his or her breath without bringing this out in the open, other members may begin to do this as well. Such issues need to be addressed openly so the negative norm does not become a hidden agenda, or a communication below the surface dialogue of the group. Hidden agendas can slow down or stop the progress of the group through the stages.

Resources

Corey, M. S., & Corey, G. (1992). *Groups: Process and practice* (4th ed.). Pacific Grove: Brooks/Cole.

Gazda, G. M. (1976). *Theories and methods of group counseling in the schools* (2nd ed.). Springfield, IL: Charles C Thomas.

Schmidt, J. J. (1993). *Counseling in schools: Essential services and comprehensive programs* (chap. 5). Boston: Allyn & Bacon.

Seligman, M. (1982). Introduction. In M. Seligman (Ed.), *Group psychotherapy and counseling with special populations* (pp. 1–23). Baltimore: University Park Press.

Tuckman, B. W. (1965). Developmental sequences in small groups. *Psychological Bulletin, 63*, 384–399.

Tuckman, B.W., & Jensen, M.A. (1977). Stages of small group development revisited. *Group and Organization, 2*, 419–427.

Vander Kolk, C. (1985). *Introduction to group counseling and psychotherapy*. Columbus: Charles E. Merrill.

Practice: Ground Rules and Other Norms

Ground Rules

> Use the process described here during the first group session to help group members establish explicit ground rules.

1. Tape a blank piece of chart paper or newsprint to a wall, or spread the paper on the floor in the center of the group circle. Define ground rules as behaviors expected in the group and explain why they are important. Encourage members to discuss what ground rules would be helpful to the group.

2. Let each child who wants to participate choose a colored marker and write out a ground rule on the paper. Some typical ground rules are as follows:

   > Come to group on time.
   >
   > Give everyone a chance to talk.
   >
   > Treat others with respect.
   >
   > No "put-downs."

3. Ask the group if they have any other ground rules that they think are necessary or helpful. Let them know that they may add to the list during the course of the group if they think of other ground rules that would be useful to the group as a whole.

Implicit Norms

> The procedure next described is a typical ice-breaker
> for a group's first session. Follow the suggestions for
> reinforcing any or all of the norms identified. Continue
> reinforcing these behaviors—and any other norms you
> wish—as the group continues.

1. Introduce yourself and welcome the children to group. Tell
   them that in this session it is important to get to know one
   another and begin to share what they want to learn in group.
   Ask them if they would be willing to participate in an "ice
   breaker" activity to get to know one another better.

2. Have children pair up with the person next to them and share
   their names, favorite food, and some thought or feeling related
   to the group topic. For example, if the group is on the topic of
   death and loss, this might concern what they would like to
   learn about themselves or something about the person they
   have lost. If the topic is family divorce, they might share one
   good thing about their new family situation.

3. After a few minutes, reconvene the larger group, then encourage
   each member to share the information he or she gained about
   the other. As group members speak, model and reinforce the
   following norms:

   > Appreciation for self-disclosure: Say something like
   > "Thank you for sharing about your partner" to each
   > child who speaks. Use your best listening skills. Watch
   > the child who is talking and smile, nod, and give other
   > nonverbal encouragement for sharing.

   > Talking to one another and not to you: When a child
   > looks at you and talks, say, in a low voice, "Would you
   > say that to the group?" Look away from the child so he
   > or she will look at and talk to the other group members.

Linking with other group members: If a child looks at you and mentions something about another group member (e.g., "Karen is sad, too") gently tell the child to address the other group member directly. For example: "Maybe Karen needs to know you recognize that she is sad. Go ahead and talk to her rather than to me. Tell Karen you think she looks sad, too."

Taking turns: If someone wants to talk a second time, say, "Could you please wait until everyone has had a turn, then you can talk again. Thanks so much."

Activities and Exercises

Overview

Activities and exercises are purposeful structured or semistructured actions designed to help group members move toward their personal goals as well as toward the goals of the group. They may include any of the following:

Movement exercises (changing chairs, dance)

Art activities (drawing a picture of one's stepfamily, making a quilt of group activities, creating a collage representing life goals or experiences, sculpting)

Go-arounds (responding to a sentence stem or predetermined question or statement, such as "How are you feeling right now?")

Ice-breakers (activities to introduce members at the beginning of the first group session)

Energizers (activities that redirect the focus of the session and reenergize the group)

Music activities (listening to music, making up songs, playing homemade instruments)

Theoretically based activities (self-improvement homework, feedback to other members)

Dyads or triads

Moral dilemma or group decision-making exercises

Activities or exercises can be carefully planned or impromptu, allowing for a range of member expression. Almost all group experiences involve the use of some type of activity or exercise at some time.

Rationale

By providing structure, activities and exercises help group members get acquainted and encourage reluctant members to connect with others in the group. A structured approach may also be required to provide experiential learning, change direction or focus in the group, reenergize the group, or make a particular point with a member or the group as a whole.

Often a ready-made topic or action designed to stimulate the group to respond in a certain way can enhance members' ability to self-disclose. Working on a common task promotes the process of building cohesion and enthusiasm for the group process.

Another reason for using exercises and activities is very obvious: Children's natural medium is play—not talk therapy! They need structured and semistructured activities where they can be creative, explore new ideas, practice new behaviors, and otherwise use their exuberant energies. The younger the children, the more activity oriented a group can be. Puppets, drawing, construction, music, and dress-up activities enhance children's learning and allow them to express their feelings.

Specific goals for the use of exercises and activities include the following:

1. To obtain information about group members

2. To increase the comfort level of members and promote interaction among them

3. To provide a fun and relaxing experience

4. To intensify certain feelings to help group members learn from them

5. To stimulate shy members to participate

6. To provide an opportunity for experiential learning ("learning by doing")

7. To provide a forum for skill development

How to Use the Skill

Activities and exercises can be thought of as being on a continuum from low to high with regard to affect and self-disclosure. It is important to select activities that fit the stage the group is in, the age and needs of the members, and the level of affect and self-disclosure that can be tolerated at the time and that can be expected to advance the group's goals. For example, an appropriate ice breaker for an initial session with a group of 8- to 10-year-old children whose families have experienced divorce would involve pairing members and having them share their names, a favorite food, and one thing they would like to learn from coming to the group. Sharing names and a favorite food involves a low level of disclosure and affect; choosing and disclosing goals for learning in the group reflect a moderate level. It would not be appropriate at this time to ask children to share the most painful thing about their parents' divorce. Asking a question requiring a high level of self-disclosure and drawing a high level of affect at the beginning of the first session might alarm low self-disclosers, and some might even drop out of group prematurely. By giving children a choice of what to say in the beginning, you structure the situation so it is not too uncomfortable.

Another "how to" aspect of activities and exercises concerns giving directions. If you give directions in a haphazard way, you are unlikely to get the desired results, and you risk confusing group members and making them less willing to participate. Here are some guidelines for giving clear and meaningful directions:

1. Keep directions simple. If there are two or three steps, give one at a time.

2. Watch the children's body language to determine if they have understood the directions. If they look puzzled, you know they haven't gotten the point.

3. Practice first. Tell a colleague that you are going to give directions for an activity in group and ask if he or she will listen to you and give you some feedback about whether your directions are clear.

4. Be sure to tell the group the purpose of the activity. If they don't know why you are asking them to do something, they will be less likely to get involved. This is especially true for homework exercises. Be sure members can tell you in their own words what the purpose is—otherwise your compliance will be very low.

5. Remember to tell group members that they have the right to say, "I pass" if they do not want to participate.

6. Tell the members how much time they have to do the activity or exercise. If you don't, they may not be able to complete the process. For example, if you are having members share information in dyads, tell them they have 10 minutes to finish the exercise so they can switch roles after about 5 minutes.

7. If the activity is conducive to it, first model the behavior. This will help group members see and hear the way the activity is supposed to be and sets them at ease. In some cases, however, modeling the behavior is not appropriate or helpful. For example, if you are working with dyads and there is an uneven number, you would usually pair up with the left-out member. However, if the children are sharing something about an experience that you have not experienced, you might choose to add a third child to one of the groups, then help the children by answering questions and encouraging them. If the children are drawing pictures of how they handle situations where they are very angry, you might best use your time by roving among and talking with them as they draw.

8. Watch for emotional reactions. Remember, even an activity that you think is low to moderate in terms of self-disclosure and/or affect might prompt a higher level emotional response in a group member because of a recent, intense experience. Be ready to respond if a child reacts strongly with anger, tears, fear, whatever. Know what you are going to do if this occurs—change or stop the exercise, remove the child, and so forth.

Finally, it is important to use activities and exercises cautiously. Each group must go through the initial, transition, and working stages. In order to get to the working stage, the group must traverse the first two stages. The members are learning new patterns, are anxious about self-disclosing and what the future holds, and frequently pose problems for other members and you by exhibiting negative behaviors. Their fear and anxiety drives acting out, resistance, irritability, negativism, and other demonstrations of underlying insecurity. Group work is hard work, for leader and members alike, and experienced as well as novice group leaders are frequently tempted to use an activity or exercise instead of permitting the natural pulls and tugs of group dynamics. It is up to you as the group leader to encourage and reinforce positive behaviors and to allow the group process to unfold. Even though it is more difficult to confront and bring negative feelings out into the open, unless you do the group cannot progress to the working stage.

Resources

Canfield, J. (1976). *100 ways to raise self-concept in the classroom.* Englewood Cliffs, NJ: Erlbaum.

Dossick, J., & Shea, E. (1988). *Creative therapy: 52 exercises for groups.* Sarasota, FL: Professional Resource Exchange.

Foster, E. S. (1989). *Energizers and ice breakers for all ages and stages.* Minneapolis: Educational Media Corporation.

Foster-Harrison, E. S. (1994). *More energizers and ice breakers for all ages and stages.* Minneapolis: Educational Media Corporation.

Peyser Hazouri, S., & Smith McLaughlin, M. (1993). *Warm-ups and wind-downs.* Minneapolis: Educational Media Corporation.

Tubesing, N. L., & Tubesing, D. A. (Eds.). (1983). *Structured exercises in stress management.* Duluth, MN: Whole Person Press.

Wenc, C. C. (1993). *Cooperation: Learning through laughter* (2nd ed.). Minneapolis: Educational Media Corporation.

Practice: Activities and Exercises

> This activity is an ice-breaker that can be used at the first session.

1. Explain that the group will be doing a get-acquainted activity to get to know one another better.

   (Stating the purpose of the activity)

2. Instruct group members to pair up, then take turns sharing:

   > Your name and what you like or dislike about it

   > What you hope to learn in this group

   > How you would complete the sentence "The nice thing about being me is_____ "

   (Giving simple directions; watching for clues to see if group members understand)

3. Let group members know that if they feel uncomfortable they don't have to participate; others will respect this decision.

   (Giving members the right not to participate)

4. Tell the pairs that they have 10 minutes for this activity, 5 for each group member. Let them know you will tell them when it is time to switch.

   (Specifying how much time the activity takes)

5. Model the activity. For example:

   > My name is Ms. D'Angelo, and I'm your group leader. What I want to learn about in this group is how it feels to boys and girls who live in a family where there has been a divorce. The nice thing about being me is that I have a lot of compassion for people and animals and the environment.

Goal Setting

Overview

Two of the major types of goals in groups are (a) the leader's goals for the group experience as a whole and for each individual session and (b) the members' individual behavior change goals. This discussion touches on helping children understand what the goals of the group and session are from the leader's perspective but focuses mainly on helping children learn how to select and pursue their own goals in terms of behavior change and skill development.

Leader Goals

Following are some general goals a group leader might have for the members of an anger management group:

> To explore the emotion of anger and what situations seem to result in aggressive behaviors

> To learn the difference between appropriate and inappropriate anger responses and see that appropriate ways to deal with anger generally have more positive consequences

> To learn some new coping skills to deal with anger

> To take personal responsibility for thoughts, feelings, and behaviors

Following are some goals the leader might have for members during the third session of that same anger management group:

> To discuss the idea that self-talk influences how we feel

> To practice developing and making coping statements

> To practice using coping statements between sessions

Member Goals

The children in a group usually have little or no experience at developing, setting, and working toward goals in a systematic way. By helping them at the pregroup interview to explore their goals for the group and by setting the norm early in the group's life that working toward goals gives direction, purpose, and a way to measure success, you can help teach the value of goals.

The following are some examples of goals a child might identify during a pregroup interview for the anger management group:

"I want to learn not to be so mad all the time."

"I want to stop getting in so many fights."

"I would like to make some friends because nobody likes me."

"I can't help getting mad and fighting."

"I am tired of getting in trouble all the time 'cause I pop off to my teachers."

Although these statements are not fully articulated, they do represent the child's understanding at the time of what is causing emotional pain. During the pregroup interview, you have the opportunity to explain what will happen in the group and what kinds of things the child can expect to learn and practice. The child can then think about what you have described. Frequently, if you ask group members to share their goals for the group at the first session, you will find that they have revised and refined what they told you during the pregroup interview. Likewise, as the group progresses and as members gain insight and practice new behaviors, you will see their goals evolve.

Rationale

Both leader and member goals provide a guideline for motivation and direction—a personal yardstick to determine whether each child is getting what he or she wants and needs from the group. Goals also provide a guideline for group behavior. Sometimes the children's behavior comes in conflict with group goals, and the situation becomes a learning opportunity for the whole group. For example, if one of the goals of the group is to learn better ways of dealing with anger and group members get into a conflict, you can help them understand that it is acceptable to disagree, to get angry with one another, to express their feelings, and to have very different values. At the same time, you can teach that it is unacceptable to act out anger by hitting or running out of group. If faced with this situation you might say, for example, "Ian, I understand that you are mad at Frankie, but you can't hit him. We need to explore some other ways for you to express your anger."

Goals also provide children with a certain sense of comfort. If they don't know why they are in the group or what they are working to achieve, the group ceases to be a safe place to explore new ways to deal with problems. Goals provide a sense of security that the group has a purpose and that you as the leader are a safe, trustworthy person who knows what to do in this new situation.

Finally, goals help both the leader and the members look realistically at what has been accomplished during the life of the group, be accountable, and take responsibility for making plans to work further after the group is over. After all, the ending of the group is really just the commencement of life after the group, and the self-exploration done in group serves not only to provide new skills and behaviors but also to raise new questions about future directions.

How to Use the Skill

In group counseling, goals are more flexible than in an instructional setting where specific skills or abilities must be mastered. As a group leader you are dealing primarily with affect and only secondarily with the learning of new skills. As a result, the goals for the group and its members will be more general—for example, becoming more aware of what we value in a friendship as opposed to completing six math problems at the end of the chapter.

Children usually come to the group with few expectations for their experience. As the group begins its journey, they will need to clarify their goals. Children are not able to deal with abstract concepts and will need assistance in being able to "guesstimate" where they are in working toward their goals. If their goals are unclear or unrealistic, they may leave the group experience feeling like failures. It is best to be flexible on this and encourage the children to pursue simple goals from session to session rather than trying to keep them focused on a major goal throughout the group. If you tend to short-term focused goals, the longer term goals will take care of themselves.

One thing you can do as group leader to help children get used to thinking in terms of goals is to model goal setting by stating the session goals each time members meet. Be clear and brief, avoiding details group members won't understand or remember. Some statements of session goals are as follows:

"The group today is going to give us time to practice responding to anger."

"Today we are going to work on learning how our behavior is what determines our reputation."

"What we are going to do today is explore some of our short-term and long-term responsibilities."

At the end of the session you could say, "I wonder what you think about whether we met the goals for this session?"

If you continue to refer to goals and guideposts, group members will learn to use them to determine whether they are moving forward or need to make adjustments. Older youths can keep a log of their goals and their progress toward them, sharing some of this information with the group. A more formal way of setting goals is to use the therapeutic technique "Contracting," discussed later in this book. You can use a standard behavioral contract, or you can have the children develop their own contracts, a process that gives them a great deal of ownership and enhances compliance.

Whatever you do, it is important to let children know that they are responsible for setting and working toward their own goals and that no one else will do this for them. The group context should then provide a safe and nurturing environment for accomplishment.

Resources

Corey, M. S., & Corey, G. (1992). *Groups: Process and practice* (4th ed.). Pacific Grove, CA: Brooks/Cole.

Rose, S. D., & Edelson, J. L. (1987). *Working with children and adolescents in groups*. San Francisco: Jossey-Bass.

Schmidt, J. J. (1993). *Counseling in schools: Essential services and comprehensive programs* (chap. 5). Boston: Allyn & Bacon.

Practice: Goal Setting

Use this activity at the first group session to help members understand that they can focus their energies to work toward the goals they choose.

1. Reproduce and give each group member several copies of the My Goal Map form (Figure 12), along with an envelope or folder to keep them in.

2. Explain the purpose of the goal map. For example:

    During the group you will have help working on your goals for change. This goal map can help you describe and plan how to get to a goal. Think of your goal as if it were a place you were going on vacation. The "stops" on the map are like the places you will visit along the way.

3. Ask the children to form dyads and discuss what they want to get out of the group experience in terms of some specific behavioral change. Have each person write this down in the space marked "Goal" at the top of the page.

4. Reconvene the whole group, then ask each member to share his or her goal. As children share, help them start thinking about what stops they will need to make along the way toward their destinations. Encourage them to fill in these steps on their goal maps, then discuss ways they could celebrate making progress toward reaching their goals.

5. Collect the goal maps and make a copy of them for your own reference. Return the originals so group members can keep them in their files and consider, change, or work on this or other goals in future sessions.

FIGURE **12**

My Goal Map

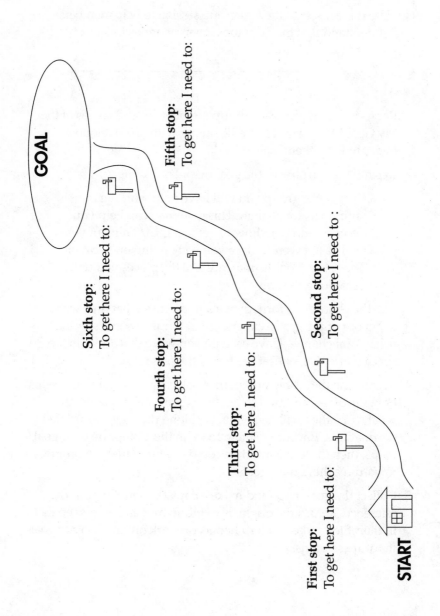

Sixth stop:
To get here I need to:

Fifth stop:
To get here I need to:

Fourth stop:
To get here I need to:

Third stop:
To get here I need to:

Second stop:
To get here I need to :

First stop:
To get here I need to:

GOAL

START

Dyads and Triads

Overview

Dividing the group into smaller groups (triads) or pairs (dyads) is an approach that has been used with adults in groups for many years. Corey, Corey, Callanan, and Russell (1992) have advocated using dyads at the beginning of a group to lessen members' feelings of intimidation. Jacobs, Harvill, and Masson (1994) have suggested using dyads at the end of the group session in order to help members summarize what has gone on during the session. In groups for children I have found the most success with dyads at the ice-breaker and review times, and with triads during the working time. The dyad and triad configurations are the most common, but dividing the group into two groups of four is also workable for some activities— for example, when having groups take opposite sides of an issue or practice a skill.

Rationale

The main purpose of using dyads and triads in the group session is to allow children to be involved in a learning activity that is less intimidating than sharing with the whole group. This is especially true for those who are not used to groups or are shy about self-disclosing. The smaller groupings help them to learn to talk about their thoughts, feelings, and behaviors in a more private way before sharing with a larger group.

Some specific goals of using subgroups are as follows:

1. To provide a more comfortable way of getting started and help children get to know one another more quickly than they could in the larger group

2. To allow children to brainstorm ideas without fear of being ridiculed

3. To accomplish certain activities (e.g., using triads to have two children practice a certain skill while the third serves as "coach," recorder, or helper)

113

How to Use the Skill

You can form the dyads or triads, or the children can select their own groupings. To have children select their own groupings, you can describe the activity, remind them of their right not to participate, then instruct them to choose their own partner or partners. You can choose the groupings randomly by, for example, having each child pair up with the person seated to the right or left. Another way to select pairs or triads at random is to have children count off, then group all the ones together, the twos together, and so forth. Finally, you can choose the groupings to achieve a particular goal—for example, pairing a low self-discloser with a moderate self-discloser so that the low self-discloser will have an appropriate model who at the same time isn't too intimidating. Or you might instruct group members to select the person they know the least in the group so that they will have the opportunity to get to know others better.

When having children work in triads, it is important to notice who chooses to practice the skills and who chooses to be the monitor or coach. Some children don't like to practice skills and need more encouragement to take an active role. When you have the triads practice a second time, be sure to tell them to let someone else be the coach/monitor so everyone gets a chance to learn the new skill.

Triads are especially helpful when you are having the group practice skills—for example, being more assertive in asking for help, responding to a bully or peer pressure, or role-playing a conflict with parents. You can have two or three triads practice the skills for 15 or 20 minutes, then come back and share what they learned with the rest of the group. Triads are also very effective when you are using the self-as-model therapeutic technique, discussed later in this book. In this technique children improve their skills by listening to or observing their own performance, either on audio- or videotape. Children who are reluctant to speak into a microphone or be videotaped with seven or eight others watching will do so readily with one or two helping and coaching.

Don't overdo the use of dyads and triads. If smaller groupings are used too often, they can detract from the total group experience. A good guideline for an eight-session topical group would be to use dyads or triads at the first session during the ice-breaker and then only once or twice more during the group experience.

Resources

Corey, G., Corey, M. S., Callanan, P., & Russell, J. M. (1992). *Group techniques* (2nd ed.). Pacific Grove, CA: Brooks/Cole.

Jacobs, E. E., Harvill, R. L., & Masson, R. L. (1994). *Group counseling: Strategies and skills* (2nd ed.). Pacific Grove, CA: Brooks/Cole.

Practice: Dyads and Triads

Follow the guidelines for conducting activities and
exercises given on pages 101–106 for all of the practice
situations.

Brainstorming

This activity is an energizer for dyads or triads, to be used
in a group to practice the skill of brainstorming or just to
reenergize the group after a heavy topic. You will need
paper and pencil for each dyad/triad and several small
items (e.g., paper clip, feather, rubber band).

1. Explain that dyads or triads will brainstorm as many uses as
possible for an item that you will hold up.

2. Hold up each item for a few minutes. Continue with different
items as time permits. (The children need to have sufficient
writing skills to do this activity in a short time.)

3. If desired, give the dyad or triad with most uses written on their
paper a small prize. You can give the rest a treat, too, for their
"super efforts."

Getting Acquainted

This exercise is an ice-breaker activity best used at the beginning of the group experience. It can be used with almost any age.

1. Pair group members and let them know that they will be doing a get-acquainted activity. Tell the children that after they have shared with each other they will get back together with the group and introduce their new friend/group member.

2. Have the pairs take turns interviewing each other, sharing name, where they feel most free to be themselves, and what they want to learn from the group. Also have them share how they would finish one of the following sentence stems:

    Elementary: "What I do best is _____ ."

    Middle school: "Something I am proud of is _____ ."

    High school: "A difficult situation I have coped with is _____ ."

3. Invite group members to make their introductions.

Go-Arounds

Overview

Go-arounds, or just "rounds," have been widely used in group work for as long as there has been group work. The skill of conducting go-arounds is helpful in all types of groups—classroom guidance, group counseling, group psychotherapy, task groups, support groups, and others. This relatively simple approach is very powerful in its ability to reenergize group members and refocus, deepen, and/or maximize what has happened in the session.

In a go-around, each member has the opportunity to respond to a specific topic, statement, or question. The lead can be in the form of an incomplete sentence, such as "Today I feel _____ about_____ ," or it can be a specific question, such as "Would you all please say what you would like to get out of this session?"

Jacobs, Harvill, and Masson (1994) describe three types of rounds: designated word or number rounds, word or phrase response rounds, and rounds requiring comment.

Designated Word or Number Rounds

In a designated word or number round, group members respond briefly by selecting from among a number of predetermined responses, either words or numbers. For example:

> "Let's have a quick go-around and ask everyone to share in just a few words how you like coming to group so far, such as 'a lot,' 'some,' or 'not very much.'"

> "Would you let us know how scary it was for you when your parents divorced by saying 'a little scary,' 'pretty scary,' or 'very scary'?"

> "I'm wondering where you are with your goals. Would each of you respond to this statement: 'Today I feel _____ about my goals.'"

"I wonder if you are learning about better ways of being angry. Would you finish this sentence so we know where you are: 'I have learned a lot/some/not much/nothing about better ways of being angry'?"

"On a scale of 1 to 10—1 meaning not at all and 10 meaning very much—how much did you get out of group today?"

Word or Phrase Response Rounds

A word or phrase response round is helpful when you need to get a reading on members without having them share at length. It prevents children from rambling or taking up unnecessary time; it also lets them know where the others are on an issue and whom they can connect with at their level of feeling. Some examples are as follows:

"Would you all go around and tell us in a couple of words what it was like for you to go to the funeral of your loved one?"

"Could each of you briefly tell us what it was like to get arrested?"

"How did it feel to get 100% on your paper—would you tell us in a couple of words?"

"What was it like to go over to the middle school and check it out? Could you tell us in a couple of words?"

Rounds Requiring Comment

Other types of rounds require that children describe or share more than just a brief statement about their feelings, behaviors, opinions, ideas, or experiences. You can ask for a more complete description by encouraging group members to choose their own way to comment:

"Would each of you share one or two things you learned in group today?"

"Could we hear from each of you on what you want to learn before the group is over?"

"What does each of you think about having a pizza at the last group session?"

"Could we hear what you're thinking about the group's coming to an end next week?"

Alternatively, you can give the group a stimulus statement or question to get them started. For example: "Now could you be more specific about *what* it is you have learned about how to manage anger? Please begin by completing this sentence: 'I have learned to deal with my anger better by _____ .' "

Rationale

Go-arounds do a number of important things. Perhaps most important, they structure the process of eliciting information from members. Some children need this structure to be able to participate. A go-around is especially useful in encouraging self-disclosure in children who have not been participating because of shyness, lack of social skills, or other reasons. You can start the go-around and let high self-disclosers go first. This allows the low self-disclosers to hear and see what a response is like before participating.

Go-arounds also provide you with essential information to help the group and its individual members move toward their goals. For example, they permit you to get a quick reading on the emotional tone of the group. You can ask the members to respond quickly to a stimulus, then focus or refocus the group in a more fruitful direction.

In addition, go-arounds can change the level of participation or insight in the group. By raising deeper questions, you can encourage members to look deeper within themselves. Using go-rounds also helps keep a group that has a tendency to ramble focused on the topic at hand.

Finally, go-arounds help children process what has happened in the group, thus maximizing the experience that they take away by allowing them to summarize and share this with the other group members.

How to Use the Skill

You can begin a go-around in several ways:

1. You can give the stimulus, then designate who is to respond first. For example, you could first model the response, then turn to your left and look at that group member, nonverbally designating him or her as the next to respond. That person usually responds, then looks toward the next person, and the go-around continues from left to right.

2. You can give the stimulus and wait for a high self-discloser to respond. Anyone else who wants to follow may do so.

3. You can give the stimulus, then instruct the group that members can respond in any order they want.

I prefer the third option because you can always count on your high self-disclosers in the group to share. Once one or two group members have shared, the rest of the group has permission to "go." In addition, this option allows low self-disclosers to watch and listen to the others without having to respond in turn. As a result, they are more tuned in to what is said and less anxious about being in the spotlight next. If you have a specific purpose for going in a particular order—for example, you want to end the experience with a certain child—then go ahead, but the self-choice method generally works best.

Try not to overuse this approach. Go-arounds are intended to intensify the experience briefly and then allow you to move on to more thorough discussion or to close the group. Kids get tired of the same approach, so use other techniques unless you have a specific purpose for using the go-around. Also, if you start a go-around, be sure you finish it! Sometimes a long-winded child will start story-telling, asking questions, or commenting to other members. Once you begin, it is your responsibility to ride herd on the process and give everyone a chance to speak.

If you have time and you want to help the children make connections with one another and enhance group cohesion, use the linking skill, described next, after the go-around. For example, you could say, "Thank you for sharing what it was like for you to go to the funeral of a loved one. While the others were sharing, did you notice that anyone's feelings and circumstances were a lot like yours—that you felt or thought the same way about it? Could you tell that person you connected with them when they shared? Go ahead and tell them."

Resources

Corey, G. (1995). *Theory and practice of group counseling*. Pacific Grove, CA: Brooks/Cole.

Jacobs, E. E., Harvill, R. L., & Masson, R. L. (1994). *Group counseling strategies and skills* (2nd ed.). Pacific Grove, CA: Brooks/Cole.

Muro, J. J., & Kottman, T. (1995). *Guidance and counseling in the elementary and middle schools* (chap. 7). Madison, WI: Brown & Benchmark.

Trotzer, J. P. (1989). *The counselor and the group* (2nd ed.). Muncie, IN: Accelerated Development.

Wubbolding, R. E. (1993). Reality therapy with children. In T. R. Kratochwill & R. J. Morris (Eds.), *Handbook of psychology with children and adolescents* (pp. 288–319). Boston: Allyn & Bacon.

Practice: Go-Arounds

Choose one or more of the examples of go-arounds and
use them during the process or review time of your
group. Adapt as necessary.

Elementary

I'd like everybody to share one thing that you learned
in group today, so we can all hear what the group means
to you.

I'm wondering how you feel about _____'s leaving
the group; would each of you say how you feel?

What is the scariest thing about sharing feelings for you?
Would each one share with us?

Could each one finish this sentence: "I feel _____ about
going to middle school next year."

Middle School

Each of you seems to have different ideas about what is
important in friendships. Could we have a quick go-around
and have you each say the one or two most important
things to you in a friend?

Everyone here has been in a family where there has been a
divorce. Let's get a reading on how well you feel you have
coped so far. On a scale of 1 to 10—with 1 meaning not at
all and 10 meaning very well—how well have you
adjusted to your parents' divorce?

How would you rate your anger at your parents at this
point, with 1 being very low and 10 being very high?

How important it is to you to have a boyfriend or girlfriend? Could we have a quick go-around and respond "not important," "a little important," or "very important"?

High School

Let's get a reading here on how important you think it is to go to college. Would each of you share in one sentence how important it is for you?

We have only three sessions left. Would you each be willing to share briefly what goal you have for the rest of the sessions?

We seem to be staying on the surface of the issue. Could we get a reading from everyone on what you think we need to move on to?

Linking

Overview

When the group begins, the members are in the initial stage. At this point in the life of the group there is no cohesion or sense of "we-ness," of being a group that has its own life, not just a meeting of individuals. The dynamic of cohesion develops through the inter-actions of members as they experience the negative and positive emotions and behaviors of the group experience. One of the major skills you will need to facilitate cohesion is the skill of linking (also called "connecting" and "joining" in the group work literature).

According to Dr. Peg Carroll, ASGW past president, author, and professional training video leader, linking is joining individuals together psychologically (Carroll & Wiggins, 1990). As group mem-bers, we do not automatically think of our problems, feelings, hopes, issues, and behaviors as experiences that other group members might also be experiencing. Rather, we tend to think that we are the only ones in the world who feel strongly about something and generally fail to realize that our experiences could have a universal aspect shared by others. Linking, then, is a way of teaching group members to empathize with other members by making a mental and emotional connection with them as they share similarities in values and experiences. Such connections are the foundation for being able to help one another reach behavior change goals and develop personal insights.

Rationale

The main purpose of linking is to foster a sense of universality, one of the major curative factors of the group experience. Universality, as discussed by Irvin Yalom (1975), is the idea that "we're all in the same boat," that we are not alone in experiencing our problems and stresses. When children come to group, they believe that their situations are unique and that no one could possibly understand how they are thinking, feeling, and behaving. This idea is at the very heart of the reason children feel so miserable about their situations— they think that no one understands them or has ever experienced anything like what they have. What I have found over and over is that experiencing other children's sharing and naming similar pains, losses, and fears lifts a tremendous burden and rekindles hope in such children. For example, a child whose family is going through a divorce frequently thinks that the divorce is at least in part his or her fault and that peers don't know how awful and horrible it is to live in that situation. When other children whose parents have divorced share how it was and is for them, they begin to develop the sense of "we-ness" that cements friendships, inspires efforts, and revives the spirit.

Another goal of linking is to move away from a continual stream of unilateral interactions from you as the leader to the members and from the members back to you. One of the strengths of group work is that the members help "cure" one another; you don't have to do all of the work. By asking linking questions, you teach group members to communicate with one another rather than just with you.

A third goal of teaching group members to link with one another is to help the members move from more superficial issues to deeper issues. Members soon learn to reinforce one another for sharing and working on their behaviors and new skills. Lower self-disclosers, shy children, or children with less developed social skills are more likely to get beyond superficial issues with modeling from other children in the group and your guidance in making mental and emotional connections among members.

Finally, by learning to connect with one another, children not only improve the quality of their group experience but also learn a skill that they can use in relationships throughout their lives.

How to Use the Skill

Children do not automatically connect with one another any more than adults do; on the contrary, they must learn to do so. It is therefore important to incorporate linking statements and questions from the very first session to establish the norm of connecting. Specific prompts like the following can help children connect with one another:

"Who else is feeling like Jamie? Tell Jamie what it was like for you."

"Who else has had the same thing happen to them? Tell Angie about it."

"Is anyone else feeling like Paul?"

"Does anyone feel the same way? Would you share with us?"

"Melissa, that must have been a scary experience for you. Does anyone else connect with Melissa on this?"

"Who connects with Mike's situation? Tell him."

You can also teach group members the following formula for expressing linking statements: "I connected with you, _____ , when you said _____ , and I felt or thought _____ ." The practice section for this skill explains more about how to do this.

It is sometimes difficult to get group members to connect with one another directly. In an adult's presence, children are more used to talking *about* one another than talking *to* one another. It will take perseverance on your part to say, each time a child directs a comment to you, "Tell Sandra what you are saying about her" or "Talk directly to Josh about his anger." Children have already learned in class to raise their hands and respond to a teacher, and habits that have been reinforced for years in the classroom are difficult to break. However, if group cohesion is ever to occur, children will need to develop the linking skill. Once they have mastered it, it will serve them well throughout their lives.

Resources

Carroll, M. R., & Wiggins, J. (1990). *Elements of group counseling.* Denver: Love Publishing.

Yalom, I. (1975). *The theory and practice of group psychotherapy.* New York: Basic.

Practice: Linking

1. Conduct an activity or exercise in which group members share some common issue, then have a go-around in which you give each person in the group the opportunity to connect with other group members. For example, if the group is about loss, each one could share something learned from going through the loss experience; if it is a group on divorce, each could share one aspect of the divorce that he or she has had a hard time accepting.

2. After the go-around, ask group members to connect with the experiences of each other by using the following formula:

> I connected with you, _____,
>
> when you said _____,
>
> and I felt or thought _____.

Responses might be something like this:

> "I connected with you, Shari, when you said your grandma died and it hurt so badly, and I felt sorry for you because my grandpa died last summer."

> "I connected with you, Gerry, when you said your mom and dad fought all the time because I thought about how my mom and dad did too before the divorce."

> "I connected with you, Alana, when you said you were angry your brother got leukemia because my cousin got cancer and died when he was 14, and I was so sad and so mad."

> "I connected with you, Phillip, when you said your dad lost his job and you had to move to an apartment because when my mom and dad got a divorce we had to leave our house with a big back yard, and I was really furious at them."

3. After a child makes such a statement, encourage the child who has received the message to say, "Thanks, that makes me feel good" or give a similar response.

Minimal Prompts and Turn Signals

Overview

Minimal prompts are verbal or nonverbal directions the leader gives to the group members to facilitate group interaction. Turn signals are nonverbal behaviors the leader uses to regulate the timing in speaking and listening roles (Duncan, 1972, 1974). In brief, these "traffic signals" control the flow of the session.

Rationale

Minimal prompts and turn signals make it easier for everyone to know what to do and to feel more comfortable with one another. If you approach a busy intersection where there is a lot of traffic, it is easier to know when to proceed if there is a traffic light than if there is a stop sign—easier if there is a stop sign than nothing at all. Having command of these skills helps you make things go more smoothly in the session.

How to Use the Skill

Minimal Prompts

Use the following kinds of positive minimal prompts to let a child know that you are listening, respect what the child is saying, and want the child to go on:

Yes.

Mm-hmm (accompanied by a nod).

OK.

Go on.

I'm listening.

Go ahead.

I see.

Turn Signals

Turn signals can function in four ways: turn yielding, turn maintaining, turn requesting, and turn denying. *Turn yielding* occurs when you are ready to stop talking, to yield your turn to a group member. You signal this intention by slowing your speech down and/or by giving a "trailer" such as "you know" or looking directly at a particular member, thus signaling that you want the group member to speak. If this doesn't work, you could nod toward the group member or even use a hand signal in the direction of the member.

The second type of turn signal is *turn maintaining*. This happens when you want to continue talking but realize that a group member or members also want to speak. You may not want to give up the floor if you are making an important point or changing the focus of the group, perhaps going from the working time to the process time. You can maintain the speaking role by avoiding eye contact with the member who wants to talk and/or by talking faster, slightly louder, or with emphasis. Be careful not do this too often, as it may prompt members to ramble on and not want to give up their own turns!

The third type of turn behavior is *turn requesting*. When you want to speak, you can signal your desire by raising your index finger slightly and perhaps sitting up a little straighter. In this way you get the attention of the speaker. You might need to do this fairly frequently with children who have a tendency to monopolize or ramble.

Sometimes you may realize that a group member wants to stop talking and have you take over. At this point, if you want the member to continue, you might use *turn denying*. You would do this by keeping your body relaxed, looking at other members, and generally sending the message that you are still interested in what the member is saying. Perhaps you want the group member to keep exploring the issue. You would let that person know nonverbally that you were "present" but avoid responding verbally.

Resources

Duncan, S. P., Jr. (1972). Some signals and rules for taking speaking turns in conversations. *Journal of Personality and Social Psychology, 23*, 283–292.

Duncan, S. P., Jr. (1974). On the structure of speaker-auditor interaction during speaking turns. *Language in Society, 2*, 161–180.

Practice: Minimal Prompts and Turn Signals

Set a goal to use each of the following minimal prompts and turn signals at least twice during a single group session.

Minimal Prompts

Mm-hmm (with head nod).

Yes, go on.

We're listening.

I see.

Go ahead.

OK (with nod).

Nod only.

Turn Signals

Turn Yielding

Slow down your speech and look at the group member you want to have speak, OR

Nod in the direction of the member you want to have speak.

Turn Requesting

Sit up straighter and look directly at the group member who is speaking, OR

Raise your index finger while looking at the speaker.

Turn Maintaining

Avoid eye contact with the speaker or speakers, OR

Talk slightly faster and/or louder.

> If you are maintaining your turn because you are going to change the focus, explain why you are not giving up the floor. For example: "We need to move on to process time now."

Turn Denying

Don't look at other members who might be trying to get the floor to speak, AND

Keep looking at the member who is speaking to let that person know you are listening, AND

Use minimal prompts to encourage the speaker to continue sharing.

Thinking, Feeling, Behaving

Overview

A movement afoot in counseling as well as medicine is "holistic" work, in which we and our clients or patients are seen as having many interrelated aspects: physical, mental, social, educational, spiritual, and emotional. These aspects are so interrelated that change in one area necessarily affects us in other areas. The three-dimensional construct of thinking, feeling, and acting proposed by such theorists as Hutchins (1979) and L'Abate (1981) is a holistic way of looking at ourselves that has implications for group counseling with children.

By the term *thinking*, we mean all of the cognitive processes that take place in the mind: recollecting, comprehending, analyzing, synthesizing, creating, imagining, reasoning, reflecting, judging, forming opinions and beliefs, and valuing. *Feelings* are complex events having both cognitive and physiological components. Anger, fear, joy, love, and other emotions are the result of our appraisal of a situation as either positive or negative. For example, if you are driving and another car sideswipes you, your brain makes an instantaneous judgment about this situation. You have a physiological stress response as well as an emotional response, which could be a combination of several different feelings—fear, anger, relief, and more. *Behaving* includes both overt actions (e.g., throwing a ball, reciting a poem, getting into an argument) and covert actions, which cannot readily be seen (e.g., a heartbeat or having a headache).

Rationale

Group counseling involves all three of these dimensions. Many groups are designed to teach thinking skills and to encourage group members to monitor negative thoughts and replace them with more positive cognitions. The group setting also involves quite a bit of talk about feelings, including identifying one's own feelings and developing empathy for others. Positive behaviors are often the focus—ways to deal with a bully, say no to peer pressure, communicate with friends and family in more effective ways, become a better friend, and so forth.

If children cannot distinguish one of these dimensions from another, they will be unable to understand many of the goals of group counseling. For example, if a child is unaware of her feelings as distinct from her thoughts, how can she receive validation for or share those feelings? If a child cannot see that his thoughts precede and deeply influence his actions, how can he change his thinking to manage anger, overcome shyness, or set and reach goals? By teaching children about these three dimensions, you ensure that all of them are talking about the same concept when the group work concerns thoughts, feelings, or behaviors.

A group for children includes many clients at different stages of cognitive development. Even in a group where all the children are of the same chronological age, there are likely to be different levels of understanding—not to mention different stages of physical, social, emotional, and educational development! One way of helping a diverse group understand the group experience is to teach them to distinguish what happens cognitively, affectively, and behaviorally.

Although children learn these concepts in the classroom, the concepts are not usually viewed as aspects of self that we can work on and change to become better at living. Nor are children asked in the classroom to get in touch with their feelings at a given moment or concerning a given situation. In our society we have done very little teaching about feelings, especially how to deal with negative feelings constructively. In fact, when you ask adults what they are feeling, frequently they will respond by telling you what they are thinking. Children do not automatically make these distinctions either.

Discriminating among thinking, feeling, and behaving can also help you as a group leader: If you are philosophically attuned to working more directly with one or another of these aspects, knowing this fact can help you balance the three in the service of your group.

How to Use the Skill

Although these are abstract ideas and children's thinking is often very concrete, most children can learn these concepts. By about third grade the average child, if given instruction, can discriminate among thoughts, feelings, and behaviors and give a feeling-word response to the question "How are you feeling about that?" I have seen it become almost a status symbol among middle school children to know about these concepts. They are excited about having this new knowledge and feel empowered by being able to express themselves more accurately and take better control of their own behavior change experience.

The practice section for this skill suggests a way to introduce these concepts in the group. Also included are three tools that you can select from to aid your instruction: the Thinking, Feeling, Behaving Diagram (Figure 13), the Feelings Chart (Figure 14), and the Name It Challenge (Figure 15). The Thinking, Feeling, Behaving Diagram graphically presents the three dimensions, thus making them easier to comprehend. The Feelings Chart gives an array of feeling-word names and faces for different emotions; it is structured so you can introduce the idea of low, medium, and high levels of feelings. The Name It Challenge presents a number of discrimination situations and asks children to identify whether they illustrate thoughts, behaviors, or feelings. The Thinking, Feeling, Behaving Diagram and Feelings Chart are appropriate for all age groups, but the discrimination examples on the Name It Challenge have been written for children at the fourth- or fifth-grade level on up and will need to be adapted to suit the cognitive and reading levels in your specific group. A sample explanation of the distinctions among the three concepts is also provided (Figure 16); this has also been written for children at the fourth- or fifth-grade level and will need to be adapted to your specific group.

Instruction in the thinking-feeling-behaving distinction can take place at the first or second session of a group experience; after the children have become familiar with the concepts, they will have a much clearer idea of what the group is all about and be better able to select behavior change goals for themselves.

Resources

Hutchins, E. E. (1979). Systematic counseling: The T-F-A model for counselor intervention. *Personnel and Guidance Journal, 57*, 529–531.

L'Abate, L. (1981). Classification of counseling and therapy: Theorists, methods, processes, and goals: The E-R-A model. *Personnel and Guidance Journal, 59*, 263–265.

Practice: Thinking, Feeling, Behaving

1. Explain what thinking, feeling, and behaving mean in a way appropriate for the developmental level of the group. Use the Thinking, Feeling, Behaving Diagram (Figure 13) and the Feelings Chart (Figure 14) as appropriate.

2. After explaining each concept, ask group members to give their own examples of each type. Have three or four group members explain the concepts in their own words. Continue to discuss until most of the children appear to understand.

3. Next ask group members to pair up and together work through the multiple-choice questions on the Name It Challenge (Figure 15).

4. After the dyads have worked through these questions, reassemble the larger group to discuss their answers.

5. Check for understanding by having each group member give you an example of each concept: thought, feeling, and behavior.

FIGURE **13** _____

Thinking, Feeling, Behaving Diagram

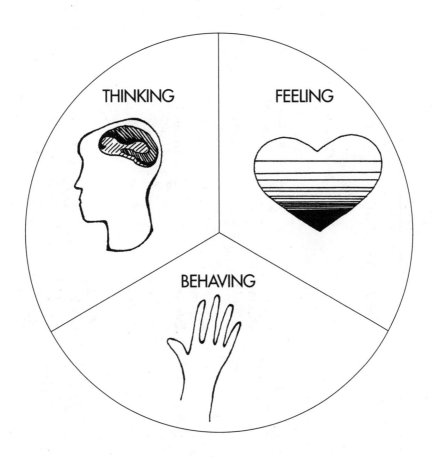

FIGURE **14**

Feelings Chart

	HAPPY	SAD	ANGRY	AFRAID
LOW	Cheerful Glad Pleased Amused Relieved	Resigned Blue Glum Gloomy Ignored	Peeved Bugged Annoyed Ruffled Cross	Uneasy Tense Anxious Nervous Puzzled
MEDIUM	Delighted Excited Bubbly Tickled Glowing	Forlorn Dejected Slighted Defeated Burdened	Disgusted Irritated Hostile Riled Biting	Alarmed Fearful Strained Shaky Jittery
HIGH	Elated Ecstatic Jubilant Overjoyed Radiant	Miserable Crushed Helpless Worthless Depressed	Fuming Furious Outraged Hateful Burned up	Panicked Horrified Terrified Petrified Desperate

Figure **15**

Name It Challenge

Write A for thoughts. Write B for behaviors. Write C for feelings.

_____ 1. Figuring out a new way to do a math problem

_____ 2. Going to the refrigerator and getting some soda

_____ 3. Getting a red face from being embarrassed

_____ 4. Dreaming about summer vacation

_____ 5. Eating ice cream

_____ 6. Being excited about your birthday party tomorrow

_____ 7. Receiving a surprise package, and you're thrilled

_____ 8. Riding your bike fast down the hill

_____ 9. Having your dad forget to pick you up to visit him, and you're disappointed

_____ 10. Thinking you are going to get a B on your report card and instead getting a D, and you are furious

_____ 11. Finishing cleaning up your clothes closet

_____ 12. Hearing that your best friend is moving far away, and you are glum

_____ 13. Trying to decide to go to the movies or play a game

_____ 14. Having the class bully take your new calculator, and you are angry

_____ 15. Wondering whether to go to college or to technical school

_____ 16. Having your boyfriend/girlfriend break up with you, and you are torn up

_____ 17. Working on finishing your homework science project

_____ 18. Being bugged because your sister has the radio on very loud

_____ 19. Deciding between red raspberry or chocolate ice cream

_____ 20. Wondering what it is like in Canada, where your friend moved

FIGURE **16** _____

Sample Explanation of
Thinking, Feeling, Behaving

Thinking

Thoughts are what happen in your mind. Lots of things happen in your mind and can be called thoughts. For example, *memories* might be remembering someone who has died, or what your friend told you before she moved, or what your dog was like before you had to give him away, or where you put your sneakers. These are things that happened in the past. Here are some other examples:

Did I put my bike in the garage, or did I leave it on the front sidewalk?

My grandma used to make the best chocolate chip peanut butter cookies in the world.

Is that bird a chickadee or a nuthatch?

Valuing is another part of thinking, and it means choosing some-thing you like more than something else, like valuing honesty rather than telling lies or valuing playing ball rather than practicing the piano. Valuing is a choice you're making in your mind, so it is part of thinking. Here are some other examples of valuing:

Do I want to have _____ for a friend?

Should I try that cigarette I was offered?

What's the best way to rearrange the furniture in my bedroom?

Working math problems and figuring things out is another part of thinking, called *reasoning*. Here are some examples of reasoning:

If I drink too much soda when I'm overheated, what will happen?

I've got to figure out how to put this toy together.

Should I take biology or music next semester?

What examples of thinking can you think of?

Feeling

Feelings are also called "emotions." Feelings are how we experience things. Feelings can be "felt"—that is, we can usually describe how our body is when we have a particularly strong feeling, such as anger, or fear, or happiness. Feelings have two parts to them, the part that takes place in your brain and the part that takes place in the rest of your body. You can learn to identify where in your body you "feel" a feeling. Where in your body do you feel anger? (You might get red in the face or feel choked up or tight-fisted.) What is it like to feel scared—where in your body do you feel the feeling of scared? (You might feel the hair on your neck prickle or get an empty feeling in your stomach.) Feelings help us know whether something is good for us or bad for us so we can take action, like run away from something frightening or share our feeling with someone when we are joyful.

Feelings are not good or bad—they are part of who we are. Sometimes when we have strong feelings, like anger, we do things that other people do not like, and we may get in trouble. What happens if you hit your brother or sister because he or she teases you and you get angry? (You might get hit back, or your parent might punish you both.) It is what you *do* with your feelings that can be good or bad. The feelings themselves are not good or bad—they are a natural part of us.

Feelings come in levels or degrees—low, medium, or high. You can choose to have just a little feeling about something, or you can choose to have a high level feeling about that same thing. When feelings get very strong, we sometimes do something hurtful to express or get those feelings out. Then perhaps we are sorry we did that hurtful thing. If we thought about it beforehand, we might not have gotten so angry and done what we did. For example, suppose your friend borrows your skates and takes a wheel off. You could choose to be bugged (low), irritated (medium), or furious (high). Instead of being furious and screaming and yelling at your friend, which will not help the situation at all and only end up with you getting in trouble, you could choose to be bugged or irritated and tell your friend how mad you are and that he or she needs to get the skate fixed.

What examples of feelings can you think of?

Figure 16 (continued)

Behaving

Behaviors are the things we do. You can see me sitting here talking to you, and I can see you writing something in your notebook. Those are behaviors. Some behaviors you can't see, such as someone's heart beating or a headache. In group we talk about behaviors a lot because sometimes we need to change our behaviors to get what we want out of life. Sometimes we learn things to do that get us in trouble or aren't good for us, and we need to learn new behaviors that are more helpful to us.

What examples of behaviors can you think of? What behaviors would you like to change about yourself?

Empathy

Overview

Every human being wants desperately to be listened to and understood. Children want to be listened to and understood also. If you ask teenagers what they dislike about adults, many times they will say, "They don't listen to me" or "They don't understand me." Empathy, then, is at the very heart of group counseling, for leader and members alike.

Empathy is the ability to recognize what is happening with another person and to communicate this understanding. It is important to realize that just understanding what another person is going through is not enough; you must be able to communicate that understanding to the other person. These two aspects of empathy are called *perceiving* and *responding*.

The empathic response itself also involves two parts: the content and the feeling. *Content* refers to the external part of the message and answers questions concerning who, what, when, where, how, or why (e.g., "What happened?" "Who was involved?"). The *feeling* is the emotion involved in the situation. It can be overt, as in the statement "I'm angry at him," or covert, not mentioned directly. Both of these parts must be present for a response to be considered empathic.

Rationale

Robert Carkhuff (1969, 1983) has identified a set of "core conditions" that counselors need to have to enhance the counseling process: empathy, warmth, respect, concreteness, self-disclosure, genuineness, confrontation, and immediacy. Empathy is the most important of these core conditions; it must be present in the counseling process for progress to take place. At some point during my two decades of teaching counselors to use empathy skills, I began to realize that children, adolescents, and adults in group counseling experiences can benefit from learning empathy skills.

There are several specific reasons to teach empathy skills to children. First, such skills empower children to help one another do the work of the group—share their own experiences and how they have worked on making changes, communicate their views and attitudes about common problems, encourage and reinforce one another as they learn new behaviors and skills, and demonstrate that they understand what others are going through. Second, by using empathy skills in the group, children learn how important it is to listen to others and how wonderful it feels to be listened to! They can transfer this awareness to situations outside the group, thus enriching their lives. Third, an empathic atmosphere sets a tone of nonjudgmental acceptance and encourages self-disclosure. When children feel they are not going to be judged or punished for sharing their painful feelings or hurtful behaviors, they are more likely to try new alternatives. As children learn to empathize with one another, their courage to work on difficult problems grows because they learn that others in the group are working on *their* problems: "If they can do it, so can I!"

The specific goal of teaching empathy skills in group is to enhance children's communication ability so that they are better able to help one another work toward their individual goals and the goals of the group. Teaching empathy skills helps children learn to be better listeners, more in touch with their own feelings, and more sensitive to the feelings of others.

How to Use the Skill

Teaching empathy skills involves explaining on the level of the group involved the concepts of "walking a mile in another person's shoes," or trying to understand how another person feels, then making a response that describes both content and feeling.

One of the best ways to teach empathy is to give group members formulas that they can learn and use until making empathic statements comes naturally in their own words. For example:

It sounds like you're _____ (feeling) because _____ (content).

You seem _____ (feeling) because _____ (content).

Are you _____ (feeling) because _____ (content)?

It seems like you're _____ (feeling) because _____ (content).

Such formulas work well with children from third or fourth grade on up. It is helpful to write the formulas on chart paper and post them permanently in the group room or area. A chart of feeling words or some other list of affective adjectives should also be on display (see Figure 14).

You don't have to go into a deep philosophical discussion of all of the aspects of empathy with children. If you provide some direct instruction and model the skill yourself, the children will pick it up. The sense of empowerment it gives children to be able to identify a friend's situation and empathize is amazing. You will also experience children's sense of joy when they receive the empathy of their peers and feel truly understood.

Resources

Carkhuff, R. R. (1969). *Helping and human relations: Vol. 1. Selection and training.* New York: Holt, Rinehart and Winston.

Carkhuff, R. R. (1983). *The art of helping.* Amherst, MA: Human Resource Development Press.

Practice: Empathy

1. Teach the concept of empathy in vocabulary that your age group will understand. The main components are as follows:

> Listening for the feeling and content
>
> Trying to understand how the other person must feel
>
> Giving a response that describes both the feeling and the content (who, what, when, where, how, or why)

For example, you might say:

> How would you like to have everyone in here really listen to what you have to say and really try to understand what is happening with you? We are going to learn empathy skills. You can use these skills both in group and outside of group. Empathy means listening very carefully to someone, trying to imagine what that person is feeling, and saying something that shows you know what happened and how the person feels. Do you know what it means to "walk a mile in someone else's moccasins"? That is a Native American saying that means you should not make a judgment about someone else's behavior unless you have been in that person's place—walked where that person has walked, so to speak. Walking a mile in someone else's moccasins means having empathy for the person.

2. Share the following formulas for creating an empathy statement:

It sounds like you're _____ (feeling) because _____ (content).

You seem _____ (feeling) because _____ (content).

Are you _____ (feeling) because _____ (content)?

It seems like you're _____ (feeling) because _____ (content).

Explain that the group will practice making empathy statements for situations, then use their own situations to learn how to make empathy statements to one another.

3. Read the empathy situations given in Figure 17, then have children practice using the formulas to make empathy statements. These situations are appropriate for third grade on up. Adapt as necessary for your group.

4. After the group has discussed these situations, have a go-around and encourage each child who wants to participate to share a personal situation. Other group members then use the formulas to give empathy statements to each child who has shared a situation.

5. Remind group members that an empathy response describes both feeling and content, and encourage them to continue making empathy statements.

FIGURE **17**

Empathy Situations

Situation 1

Michelle has just learned that her mom and dad are going to get a divorce. They have told her that she is going to live with her Aunt Carol for a few months until everything gets settled.

Michelle is crying when she tells you this. Can you think of an empathy statement for Michelle?

Situation 2

Boswell is 8 years old. His dad bought him a retriever puppy for his birthday. Bos took his puppy, Treeber, for a walk every day, fed him twice a day, gave him fresh water, and played with him after school. Bos was very responsible about taking care of his special friend. One day Bos came home from school, and Treeber had dug a hole under the fence and run away. Bos was horrified and combed the neighborhood for Treeber. He looked everywhere, and his mom helped him call the animal rescue league to see if they had picked up Treeber. Bos made signs and put them up in the neighborhood, but no Treeber.

Bos has just come to school and told you this, and he is very, very upset. Can you think of an empathy statement for Bos?

Situation 3

Shazia and Raza are brother and sister. Their mom and dad came to the United States years ago from India. They live in a large city and go to Bellweather Middle School. One day they came home from school, and their mom and dad were both at home—this was very strange because both of their parents worked. Their parents told them that their grandmother in India was very ill and that their mother would have to go back to India to care for their grandmother for an unknown amount of time.

Raza and Shazia are very upset about their mother's leaving and not knowing how long she will be gone. Can you think of an empathy statement for them?

Situation 4

Pedro got a new bicycle for his birthday. His dad told him to be sure to put it in the garage every night before bedtime. One night Pedro and his friends were playing on another street, and he forgot about putting his bicycle away before he went to bed. The next morning he got up, remembered his bike, and went to get it. It was gone!

Pedro tells you about this on the bus to school. Can you think of an empathy statement for Pedro?

Situation 5

Carmen is a 13-year-old girl who lives at home with her mother and four little brothers. Her mom works three jobs to get enough money for the family. Carmen wants to be a junior high school cheerleader, but she has to take care of her brothers after school, so she can't practice the cheers she will need to learn for the tryouts. She asked the teacher who is cheerleader sponsor what to do. The teacher gave Carmen a videotape of the cheers so she can practice every day at home. When it came time for the tryouts, Carmen earned a place on the pom-pom team. Was she ever happy!

Carmen runs up to you in the hall at school to tell you she made the team. Can you think of an empathy statement for Carmen?

Questioning

Overview

Group work calls for advanced questioning skills. Questions, sometimes called "probes," are of several types. Depending upon the type of information you want, you can choose from among closed-ended, open-ended, indirect, and nonverbal or paraverbal questions.

Closed-ended questions are useful when you need to find out specific information, such as "Did you take your medication today?" or "Which classroom are you in this afternoon?" Closed-ended questions typically call for a yes-or-no answer or a very short response. They are frequently used in the classroom when children are learning content or being tested. Examples of this type include the following:

Is your mother at home?

Did you lose your pencil?

Were you on the playground at noon?

Was that dog loose?

Are your parents divorced?

Open-ended questions are generally most appropriate for group counseling because they invite elaboration. For example:

What were you feeling when you heard your mom and dad fighting?

Could you tell me more about that?

Would you give me an example?

Who could you ask for more information on that?

What have you tried to do to help yourself?

What would you be willing to do to change things?

Would you share with us what you thought about when you heard the news?

How are you feeling about that?

Indirect questions are a type of open-ended inquiry, in statement form, that facilitates a comfortable environment for self-exploration. For example:

Explain a little bit about that.

Tell us some other ways you could handle that.

Describe how you could change things.

Describe some ways you could deal with the situation if you can't change it.

I'd be interested in what you would share about this.

I wonder what you would be willing to do to make things better.

Nonverbal or paraverbal questions can also be used; in these, a quizzical look or particular tonal quality conveys the fact that a response is expected.

Rationale

Questions in the counseling process are used when you want to obtain information from group members. Specifically, a question or probe is used when you want to do the following:

Open a discussion

Encourage group members to elaborate on or continue discussing an issue

Motivate brainstorming to gather options

Help members identify specific thoughts, feelings, or behaviors, or examples of these

Help members understand a certain viewpoint

Assist group members in exploring what is happening in their lives

Although the goal of using questions is to elicit information, in a group counseling situation questions are generally asked not to elicit content-oriented information but rather to encourage self-exploratory behavior on the part of group members.

How to Use the Skill

To a certain extent, the use of questions in the educational context has left children with the impression that there is a "right" answer to questions and that if they are just smart enough or can guess well enough they will get the "right" answer. But group counseling is not primarily content oriented. Because the goal of group work is to explore and then learn new, more adaptive ways of thinking, feeling, and behaving, you will want to use mostly open-ended questions. Open-ended questions invite group members to explore their thoughts, feelings, and behaviors. These questions encourage reflection on what is going on internally rather than externally. In order to answer, children must really stop and think. I particularly like statements of exploration beginning with "I wonder." I call these "Columbo" statements, after the famous television detective who would mutter an "I wonder" statement under his breath to an unsuspecting guilty party.

In contrast, closed-ended questions set up an atmosphere of interrogation in which children may become defensive and respond quickly in order to stay in the passive role. This is not what you want to have happen! You want to encourage children to think independently and responsibly, to take action to become more self-directed. Closed-ended questions usually start with some form of the verbs "to be" or "to do" ("Are you" or "Do you"). The complexity of dealing with many young clients at once, coupled with trying to keep oneself centered and available emotionally, creates a strain and requires extra energy. If a great deal is going on in the group, it is easy to revert to asking closed questions. Closed-ended questions are easy to use but do not provide opportunities for children to self-explore.

Like closed-ended questions, "why" questions tend to put children on the defensive. The only answer to a "why" question is "because": because she told me to, because he hit me first, because he said it was OK, because I didn't think just one would hurt me—because, because, because. The result is that the child blames others or situations for his or her problems instead of taking personal responsibility for them. Like closed-ended questions, "why" questions should be avoided.

Resources

Carkhuff, R. R. (1969). *Helping and human relations: Vol. 1. Selection and training*. New York: Holt, Rinehart and Winston.

Carkhuff, R. R. (1983). *The art of helping*. Amherst, MA: Human Resource Development Press.

Carkhuff, R. R., & Anthony, W. A. (1979). *The skills of helping*. Amherst, MA: Human Resource Development Press.

Corey, M. S., & Corey, G. (1992). *Groups: Process and practice* (4th ed.). Pacific Grove, CA: Brooks/Cole.

Cormier, W. H., & Cormier, L. S. (1991). *Interviewing strategies for helpers* (3rd ed.). Pacific Grove, CA: Brooks/Cole.

Doyle, R. E. (1992). *Essential skills and strategies in the helping process*. Pacific Grove, CA: Brooks/Cole.

Jacobs, E., Harvill, R., & Masson, R. (1994). *Group counseling: Strategies and skills* (2nd ed.). Pacific Grove, CA: Brooks/Cole.

Trotzer, J. P. (1989). *The counselor and the group* (2nd ed.). Muncie, IN: Accelerated Development.

Practice: Questioning

Practice using the following open-ended questions in a group session. Note the different kind of responses that you begin getting. If the children look at you with that "What did he or she say?" look on their faces, give them an example of something that might be said in response to the question.

1. What is it like for you to _____?

2. What could you do about _____?

3. What have you tried?

4. What would you like to have happen?

5. What would you have to lose if you _____?

6. What were/are you feeling?

7. What would you do differently if _____?

8. What were you aware of when that happened?

9. What makes it difficult for you to _____?

10. What were you surprised about when _____?

11. What would you be willing to try this week?

12. How do you feel about _____?

13. Could you tell us more about that?

14. Would you share some of your feelings with us?

15. Could you give us an example of _____?

16. Would you share with us what you thought when _____?

17. How are you feeling about that?

18. Could you tell us some other ways to handle that?

19. Could you explain a little more about that?

20. How could you change this situation?

Processing

Overview

In my estimation, the skill of processing is, along with empathy, one of the most important skills a group counselor can have. Processing is a specific skill, not to be confused with the idea of group process, which refers to the stages a group goes through on its life journey.

In this context, processing is an activity initiated and conducted at the end of each group counseling session and at the end of the group experience. Processing at the end of each group session involves asking certain stimulus questions on a number of different levels, or areas of inquiry, so group members can maximize their experience. Processing at the end of the group experience involves asking stimulus questions to cover the learning experiences for all of the previous sessions so that, as the group ends, members have the opportunity to review what they have learned and clarify what they need to work on in the future.

This discussion focuses on processing at the end of each group session; for more about processing at the end of the group experience, see the discussion of "Closing Rituals" in Section 3.

Rationale

Suppose you were taking a course at the local university, and you had a final exam coming up on Monday night. You sit down Saturday morning to study for your exam and open your textbook, but someone has torn out all of the study questions at the end of the chapters! You feel angry, panicky, anxious, and aggravated. Why? Because those study questions at the end of the chapters focus on topics, issues, vocabulary, and concepts that are extremely helpful in studying for the test. They help maximize the learning experience of studying. Test questions are likely to come from those review pages, and you don't have time to reread all the chapters to figure out what information is most important.

Processing at the end of a group session is like a study review in that it helps maximize the learning experience. Specifically, processing helps children do as follows:

1. Review what the session invited them to think about

2. Review what feelings were brought to the surface, experienced, or talked about

3. Review what behaviors or skills they are working on and what progress they are making toward behavioral change

4. Articulate what they learned from the session from their own work and from other group members

5. Articulate what they are willing to do between the sessions to continue learning and working

6. Articulate other ways of using what they learned

Processing at the end of a session also helps motivate and remind group members to keep on working on their issues between sessions, empowers members by increasing their confidence in their ability to make changes in themselves, and serves as a reinforcement to those who are making progress.

How to Use the Skill

As discussed in Section 1, the group session in structured in three parts: the ice-breaker or review, the working time, and the process time. The working time is the longest, with a shorter period at the beginning and end for ice-breaker or review and processing. It will be important to use your cutting-off and focusing skills to transition from the working time to the process time, making sure that you have saved enough energy for this important aspect of group work. (Cutting-off and focusing skills are discussed later in this section.)

Processing involves questioning at four levels to help you and group members review not only the content of the session, but also the affective, behavioral, and cognitive processes that took place during the session. These four levels concern the intrapersonal dimension; the interpersonal dimension; new thoughts, feelings or behaviors; and use or application of new knowledge. For each of the levels you can select one or more questions appropriate to the age and cognitive level of the children involved. If time is short, you might want to choose only one question from each processing level.

Intrapersonal Dimension

The intrapersonal dimension concerns what went on inside the group member, including cognitions, feelings, physical reactions, and so forth. The following questions tap this level:

How did you feel about sharing with the group?

What feelings did you have when you were sharing or when other members were sharing?

What were you thinking about while others were sharing?

Interpersonal Dimension

The interpersonal dimension relates to what went on between and among the members—the relationships in the group. Sample questions at this level are as follows:

What did you see happening in the group?

What did you learn about the other group members?

What feelings or behaviors did you notice?

New Thoughts, Feelings, or Behaviors

Questions pertaining to new thoughts, feelings, or behaviors include the following:

What did you learn in group today?

What new ideas came up in group today?

What new skills or behaviors did you find out about?

What feelings do you have now that are different from when you came to the group today?

What pleased/upset you about group today?

What surprised you about group today?

What will you do differently as a result of coming to this session?

Use or Application of New Knowledge

To inquire about children's future use or application of new knowledge, these questions may help:

> What are you willing to work on this week? (Ask for a commitment to a specific task, such as meeting new friends, being assertive, asking for help, etc.)
>
> From what you learned in group today, what could you use this week to help you change your feelings (behavior, negative thoughts, etc.)?

Many group sessions are very short, and sometimes it seems that there isn't enough time to process. Yet if this is not done, you might as well not have conducted the preceding parts of the session because the children will forget a large part of what happened. The process time helps pull together all that went on so group members leave the session—and the whole group experience—with a clearer idea of what happened. The members should be able to walk out the door of the group room and say, "I learned this, this, and this, and I'm going to do this." If you don't leave time for processing, you rob the children of the opportunity to maximize their learning experience. Group time is very precious—use every minute of it with an eye toward maximizing that experience.

Practice: Processing

This value-sharing activity can be done as an ice-breaker at the first session or at a subsequent session. Allow 10 to 15 minutes for the activity, plus a process time of 6 to 8 minutes. Follow the guidelines for using activities and exercises given on pages 101–106.

1. Ask group members to share with the group something that they value. They can share something they have in their possession (e.g., picture of a new baby, special coin, ring from grandma, new sneakers, Mickey Mouse watch, favorite hair bow), or you can ask them before the session to bring something they value from home.

2. Have a go-around and let each child share whatever he or she would like with the other members. As the group members share, encourage them to connect with one another. (See the discussion of the linking skill earlier in this section.)

3. Process the activity by using the following questions.

Intrapersonal Dimension

What was it like for you to share about your special item in group?

What were you thinking or feeling while waiting to share?

Interpersonal Dimension

What did you notice the other group members doing?

What feelings or behaviors did you notice going on?

What was it like for you to be a group member?

New Thoughts, Feelings, or Behaviors

What new ideas or ways of doing things did you learn from the group?

How do you feel now as compared to the beginning of the group?

What surprised you about the session today?

What upset/pleased you about the group today?

Use or Application of New Knowledge

How can you apply what you have learned and practiced in group?

What are you willing to work on between this week and next week?

Cutting Off

Overview

Your parents told you that it was rude to interrupt—to cut people off. And yet you must master this skill to ensure positive outcomes in your group! The term "cutting off" has been used widely, especially by Jacobs, Harvill, and Masson (1994), to mean a necessary stopping of the conversation for many different legitimate reasons, not a rude interruption that would be punitive to the speaker. Cutting off has also been referred to in the group counseling literature as "blocking" (Trotzer, 1989), and "intervening" (Dyer & Vriend, 1980).

Rationale

Cutting-off skills are important because if a member talks on inappropriately and no one does anything about it the group can easily get "stuck." Some children, especially young children, have a tendency to talk on and on and not get to the point. When they get in group, this kind of conversation takes up valuable time, and the other children get bored and turned off to the group. Other children seem to need an audience so badly that they hurriedly move from one topic to another, as if they can't get everything said in time, and are soon off the subject of the session. Older children sometimes get involved in giving inaccurate information on topics of interest, such as what birth control methods are the most effective; how smoking, drugs, or alcohol affect the quality of life; or how many credits are needed to graduate from high school. They learn a little about a topic and suddenly become experts—sometimes their inaccurate information must be corrected.

It might be uncomfortable for you as a leader to have to interrupt, but you have a perfectly good reason for not being "polite" by letting group members ramble on. Since our ethical guidelines indicate that the leader is responsible for ensuring positive group outcomes, it is up to you to cut off the member who is rambling, inaccurate, arguing, storytelling, or whatever.

How to Use the Skill

The act of cutting off must be done in a thoughtful manner and followed up by certain actions or consequences. It also needs to be done at the appropriate time so that a child who is sharing something important to him- or herself and to the group's purpose is not cut off inadvertently. Jacobs et al. (1994) list seven times when it is appropriate for the leader to cut off comments by a group member. I have added numbers 8 and 9, which are especially appropriate when working with children.

1. When a member is rambling off the topic
2. When a member's comments conflict with the group's purpose
3. When a member is saying something inaccurate
4. When you want to shift the focus
5. When it is near the end of the session
6. When members are arguing
7. When members are rescuing
8. When a member is giving a moral judgment about another member's behavior
9. When a member starts storytelling about other members of the family or friends outside the group

If you cut a group member off, be sure to tell the child *why* you are interrupting. Doing so can help keep the child from misunderstanding what is happening, becoming hurt or angry, or losing confidence in you and the group experience. For example:

"Jeremiah, I need to stop you here because you are rambling off the topic. What else do you have to say about this topic?"

"Janet, let's stop here for a minute. I think the information you have about birth control is inaccurate, and we need to have accurate information here so people can make good decisions."

"Thanh, I need to stop you here because our working time is up and we need to process what we did in the group today."

"Carmen, we need to hear from the rest of the group members on this go-around, so would you please finish what you were saying."

"Tonya, we need to listen for Michael's feelings and not make judgments about whether what he did was right or wrong."

Be sure to use a warm, positive tone of voice so that the child does not think that you are angry. It takes some children who are shy and/or low self-disclosers time to build confidence to talk in group, so be careful not to cut them off when they are giving a legitimate comment. Even if a child has a history of rambling or monopolizing, it still pays to be careful. You might cut that person off just as he or she is starting to share the first really important comment of the day!

It is important to know what you are going to do once you cut off a group member. Jacobs et al. (1994) identify four choices: (a) let the person who was cut off continue, (b) move on to another person, (c) move on to another topic, and (d) move on to another activity, exercise, or part of the session. I use my personal experience while traveling in England to remind me to make sure I know what I am going to do after I cut someone off. In England, four-way stops at intersections do not exist. Instead, you get on a rotary, drive in a circle, then exit in whatever direction you want. If you don't know which road you are supposed to get off on to continue your journey, you could be stuck going around the rotary for some time. This can be especially difficult if you are just learning to drive on the right-hand side of the car and the left-hand side of the road! Before you get to the rotary, you need to determine where you want to end up. In group counseling, when you cut off a group member, you need to have decided where you are going immediately afterward—to another person, topic, activity, or back to the same person.

The following practice section suggests a focused activity, but opportunities abound to use this skill in nearly every group situation. If the activity described does not fit in with the purpose of your group, concentrate instead on using cutting-off skills during the course of your group's regular sessions. You could even practice your cutting-off skills in planning committees, faculty meetings, and the like!

Resources

Carroll, M. R. (1985). Critical issues in group work in education: Now and 2001. *Journal for Specialists in Group Work, 10*(2), 98–102.

Dyer, W., & Vriend, J. (1980). *Group counseling for personal mastery.* New York: Sovereign.

Jacobs, E. E., Harvill, R. L., & Masson, R. L. (1994). *Group counseling strategies and skills* (2nd ed.). Pacific Grove, CA: Brooks/Cole.

Trotzer, J. P. (1989). *The counselor and the group* (2nd ed.). Muncie, IN: Accelerated Development.

Practice: Cutting Off

The topic of this activity, pros and cons of drug use, is
a good choice for groups of children from about sixth
grade on. Younger children respond well to a discussion
of alternative ways to express anger.

1. Write one of the following instructions on separate 3 x 5 cards:

   Ramble off the topic.

   Make a moral judgment about what is being said.

   Start an argument with others.

   Give inaccurate information.

   Tell a long-winded story.

   Make enough cards so that three or four of the group members
   can have one.

2. Explain that the group will be doing an activity to help them
   learn that the group's time is limited and that it is important to
   stay on topic. If group members don't stay on the topic, you
   will interrupt them so they can return to it.

3. Give an index card to three or four group members. Tell them
   they are to follow the instructions on their cards after the group
   gets going.

4. Initiate a discussion about the risks and benefits of using drugs.
   (As a positive aspect, someone might say, "Well, I have asthma,
   and I use an inhaler. If I didn't have it I would have bad asthma
   attacks, so it is a good kind of drug to use.")

5. As the discussion continues, the group members will begin making statements that will require you to use your cutting-off skills. Be sure to remember to give a reason for your redirection whenever possible and to phrase your requests in a kind way.

6. Process the activity when you are finished by asking what it was like to be cut off, told why, then directed to continue in the same or another direction. You will find that the group members will learn the cutting-off skill, too!

Drawing Out

Overview

Children refrain from participating in group for many reasons. A skillful leader knows how to invite a child to take the risk of self-disclosing without being punitive or authoritarian. "Drawing out," the term used by Jacobs, Harvill, and Masson (1994) as well as others, means to encourage participation by a group member who is not sharing, for whatever reason. The problem has been addressed by other group counseling authors, mainly under the issue of dealing with silence or nondisclosure. Drawing out means inviting group members to become active, with the intended result being that they begin to participate actively in the group.

Rationale

Group work requires the full participation of all members in order to have a rich flow of ideas, sharing of feelings, and models of behavior for everyone. If only some members participate in this sharing, the children are robbed of the material needed for the group process to take place. Self-disclosure provides the energy for making connections and generating trust, cohesion, and universality. It is up to you as the group leader to deal with children who are afraid to speak, have inadequate social skills, or are shy by nature—to draw them into the process in warm and inviting ways.

How to Use the Skill

The following specific guidelines for drawing members out concern the use of indirect approaches, direct approaches, activities and exercises, warmth (nonverbal caring), and silence.

Indirect Approaches

It is generally best to begin with indirect approaches like the following:

> "We haven't heard from a couple of you yet. Would you like to share something on our topic of _____?"
> (Quickly glance at members and then look away.)

"We'd like to hear what the rest of you have to say."

"If you're comfortable, would some of you who haven't talked yet like to say something?"

Direct Approaches

If a child does not respond to an indirect invitation to participate, you can use more direct approaches. For example:

"Lashana, I'm wondering what you'd like to share about your parents' divorce situation."

"Suzanna, we'd like to hear what thoughts or feelings you have if you feel comfortable sharing."

"Jesse, what did you learn about the rest of the kids and their divorce problems?"

"Jake, I'm wondering what I can do to help you be more comfortable in the group. Would you share some of your ideas with us?"

Activities and Exercises

Activities and exercises can also help reluctant group members feel comfortable participating. You can pair or otherwise group non-participating or silent members with those who are sharing appropriately so the nonparticipants will feel more comfortable and learn from role models. You can also have children make drawings, collages, murals, or signs/slogans to represent the group or engage in some other creative activity where they must cooperate to complete the task. Go-arounds can help give everyone a chance to get hidden agendas, negative feelings, or fears of other members or of you out in the open. For example:

"I'm wondering about how scary it is to talk in group. Could we have a go-around about what you think is the scariest thing about sharing in group?"

"If I didn't come to group next time, what would you tell the rest of the group about what leaders should be like?"

"Who in the group would you most like to sit beside and work with? Who would you *not* like to sit beside and work with?"

You can follow up this last question by asking, "What do you need to feel comfortable enough to sit beside and work with _____?" This issue of trust could cause children some discomfort but needs to be dealt with; if it isn't resolved, a negative undercurrent may prevent the group from working.

Warmth (Nonverbal Caring)

Use positive body language when you invite the member to share. Look at the person and smile, nod, and lean toward the person a little. You can also look directly at the person you are speaking to. Shifting your eyes away after about 5 seconds will give the child a chance to decline and reduce the chance that he or she will become embarrassed, fearful, or resentful. It might help to sit beside the silent member as long as you can keep good eye contact with the rest of the group or pair up with the child so you can give encouragement and share what the child has said to you with the others.

When the child is shy and quiet by temperament and/or lacks social skills and experience, invite participation very gently. Use linking skills when you sense that the child wants to talk but is afraid of something, such as another member, being ridiculed, or having his or her problem or situation be perceived as being too "different" from others'. For example, you might say, "Gail, who else in the group seems to have feelings like yours?" Then when the child responds, say, "Could you go ahead and tell Maddy that you link with her and her (hurt, angry, sad, afraid) feelings?"

Silence

Drawing-out skills are essential for every group leader, but they are not the skill of choice for every silence situation. As experienced group leaders know, even during periods of silence the nonparticipating child is learning from others. Some children eventually say openly what they have learned during their silence; with others you might see a change in behavior or attitude that indicates they have been taking in what has been going on. Still others change in ways noticed by parents or teachers, who will later mention this to you in passing conversation.

Depending on the reason the child is not participating, you may choose to leave the child alone, allowing more time for the child to become comfortable, figure out what is going on, learn from others' modeling, and/or let go of some resistance by being accepted as he or she is. Some specific times when it may be best to permit the child to remain silent are as follows:

1. A child may have committed to doing self-improvement homework between sessions but not follow through. Children sometimes have a difficult time remembering to practice, or there are circumstances in their environment that are punishing and not conducive to practice, or they are not committed, or they don't know what to do or what skill to practice well enough to attempt out-of-group practice. At this time it is best not to put the child on the spot because it will only cause the child to feel uncomfortable—possibly like a failure.

2. If the child is openly resistant to being in the group and remains silent as a form of resistance and manipulation, it seems to work better to pair this child with a high-status child who is participating—in other words, one that the silent, resistant child might connect with and have a positive experience with in a dyad. You don't have to do all the work yourself; you can let other group members share responsibility for working together.

3. Sometimes a child is seriously disconnected from his or her feelings and is simply unable to share. The child is already in the group experience but has had such serious problems or life experiences that he or she is unable to deal with them, and thus sits there silent and withdrawn, out of touch but in great pain. This child might best be terminated from the group and seen in individual therapy involving techniques such as play therapy and drama to experience some emotional release.

Sometimes a member is being silent because he or she has the need to be invited several times in order to feel that it is all right to participate. For the most part, though, children need to get the idea you and other group members want them to participate, but that if they choose not to they will still be accepted. If you encourage sharing in ways that do not scare, threaten, or alienate, but rather provide the opportunity to have a positive experience and be reinforced for doing so, children will likely repeat the disclosing behavior in the future. You want each child to share on a continuing basis and eventually get beyond a superficial level of communication so everyone will be enriched by that individual child's personal feelings, thoughts, and behaviors.

In conclusion, drawing-out skills must be used in a sensitive manner. I concur with Dr. Peg Carroll, who says, "There are no easy solutions to dealing with the silent member in the group" (Carroll & Wiggins, 1990, p. 59). If the experts in the field describe silence as a difficult aspect of group work, then we can take some comfort in knowing that our struggles are validated.

Resources

Carroll, M. R., & Wiggins, J. (1990). *Elements of group counseling: Back to the basics*. Denver. Love Publishing.

Jacobs, E. E., Harvill, R. L., & Masson, R. L. (1994). *Group counseling strategies and skills* (2nd ed.). Pacific Grove, CA: Brooks/Cole.

Trotzer, J. P. (1989). *The counselor and the group* (2nd ed.). Muncie, IN: Accelerated Development.

Practice: Drawing Out

Try any or all of the following ideas in an ongoing group.

1. In a group where you have at least two members who are not participating, try saying something like the following: " _____ and _____ , I've noticed that you haven't shared your ideas yet today. I'd really like to hear what you have been thinking about because it will help me and the rest of the group understand you better. Would you share your ideas?"

2. Pair the silent member(s) with moderate to high self-disclosers in dyads, and have them share (a) the best or most helpful thing that they have learned in group so far, (b) how it has helped them, and (c) what they still want to get out of the group before it is over. Be sure to tell them that they are going to come back and share their own ideas with the larger group.

3. Write one of the following questions on a chalkboard or chart paper, then have a go-around in which group members respond to it:

> Two things I think are important about (topic of group/session) are _____ .
>
> Something that scares me about (topic) is _____ .
>
> Three things I want to learn about (topic) are _____ .
>
> What I want to be sure to learn in group is _____ .
>
> What I like the best about coming to group is _____ .
>
> What I think would happen if I shared something scary is _____ .

4. Pair the silent member(s) with children who are moderate to high self-disclosers. Give all of the children a choice of hand puppets, or have them make puppets with paper bags, then instruct them to have their puppets tell their partners what they are afraid to say in group. Be sure you tell the group ahead of time that they won't have to share this information with the rest of the group. Then get the group back together and talk about what it was like for children to share through the puppets without having to say their painful feelings to anyone else at this time.

Focusing

Overview

Focusing is the skill of knowing what is happening in the group at any particular time and being able to control and change what is happening for the benefit of all the members. Focusing the group's energies is like directing traffic—you are keeping watch over what is happening, what is coming and going, what needs to wait and what needs to move, and when to give the signal to change the flow of events. Without a calm, knowledgeable traffic director, the group becomes a mess of thoughts, feelings, and behaviors, like a honking jam of cars at an intersection.

The focus of a group session can be on any one of three contents: (a) an activity or exercise, such as an icebreaker activity or go-around; (b) any member of the group (child or leader); or (c) a specific content, such as what is it like to be in a family that experiences divorce. Focusing also goes on in three different processes, which the leader controls as the needs of the group and session timing dictate: (a) starting the focus, (b) shifting the focus, and (c) holding the focus.

Rationale

Focusing skills give you control of the flow of the session and help you facilitate the therapeutic work. It stands to reason that if you don't know what the focus is or how to manage it, a great deal of time and energy will be wasted. In group work with children, you are usually dealing with time-limited, topic-driven sessions of restricted scope, and wasted time lessens the chances that the children will profit from the sessions. All this makes focusing skills essential.

The specific goals of focusing are to control the energy of the group by managing what to focus on, whom to focus on, and when to change the focus for the benefit of the group. Each aspect of the process of focusing (starting, shifting, and holding) is associated with different goals. *Starting the focus* means establishing the direction of the session or section by telling the group members what to do, what to think about, or what issue or subject to discuss. It can also mean describing an activity or exercise that will be used to bring about a healing experience.

Shifting the focus means shifting energies directed in one way to another. Jacobs, Harvill, and Masson (1994) describe the directions in which change can take place as follows:

From a topic to a person ("Let's finish talking about your practice and go on to what Jeremy wanted to say about his dad and mom getting back together.")

From a topic to an activity ("We've talked about funerals for a long time now and have heard from everybody. Let's go to the art materials and draw with markers and crayons what the funeral looked like to you.")

From topic to topic ("I think we need to finish our brainstorming activity and discuss what we have accomplished during the session.")

From an activity to a person ("Now that we've finished brainstorming different ways to express anger, which way do you think would work best for you, Andrea?")

From an activity to a topic ("Could you finish your listing of pros and cons of drug use and focus on sharing what you think?")

From a person to an activity ("Josh, if you've finished the important part of what you wanted to say, we need to move on now and process what happened for all of us in group today.")

From a person to a topic ("Kim, I need to stop you here because you are rambling and we need to talk about the topic of abuse yet today.")

From a person to a person ("Lee, thank you for sharing about your stepfamily. Rosie, how about your stepfamily— would you have something to share?")

The goals of shifting the focus can be to reenergize the group, to move to a different topic or activity or person because the focus has been on one area for too long, or to move from one section of the group to another, such as from the review to the working time or from the working time to the process time.

Holding the focus means keeping everyone on track with the topic, issue, or whatever is happening—not letting the children stray from the topic or activity or the person who is talking. The goal is to keep on the issue at hand until it is sufficiently covered or dealt with.

How to Use the Skill

To beginning group leaders, the skill of focusing may seem difficult if not impossible. It is very confusing to begin the session with a particular topic to discuss or direction to move in and have a group member come to the session with very different needs at the moment. What do you do—go with the needs of the moment and let the group's energies shift to the child, stay with the topic planned, or perhaps go ahead with a planned activity that will help everyone focus in on the issue? What do you *focus on*—that is, what do you deal with or direct your and members' energies toward at any given time? The following guidelines for starting, shifting, and holding the focus will help you learn how to use this skill smoothly.

Starting the Focus

Start the focus through direct instruction. For example:

> Beginning the session: "Our topic today is what is important in a friendship between boyfriend and girlfriend. Could we have a go-around with each person sharing what you think are the most important things for this type of friendship to grow?"

> Starting working time: "That was a good review of what happened last week, and it seems like several of you are practicing stress management skills. Let's focus now on the working time, on how stress affects our health."

> Starting process time: "Let's focus now on what we learned in group during working time. What did you learn that you would be willing to practice this week between sessions?"

In addition to statements like these, you can use activities or exercises to start the focus. Art or creative projects, musical instruments or songs, and paper-and-pencil activities such as fill-in-the-blanks, short sentence completion, and listing of pros and cons are some ideas. To use these techniques to start the focus, you might say:

"We have a lot of art materials here today. Choose what you would like to draw or create or sculpt to show what anger looks like to you."

"Today we are going to use music to express stressful feelings. Find an instrument or song that can help you show the rest of us how you can get rid of stress and learn to relax."

"Our topic today is the pros and cons of using drugs. On the pieces of newsprint taped to the walls, take a marker and write down what you think are some of the positive and negative uses of drugs. Then we'll talk about what we have discovered."

Shifting the Focus

Shift the focus by saying something to indicate clearly that children are going to stop doing something they have been doing and start doing something else. Such specific verbal communications help everyone get readjusted. Children are used to having a bell ring or some other external event take place to signal the end of one activity and the beginning of another, so changing focus in the group in this way will be familiar to them.

With younger children or children who have problems focusing for very long, you will need to keep topics or activities short and clearly indicate the purpose for the change—for example: "Now we are going to stop drawing and come sit down in the circle so we can share what we drew and learn from each other." Another caution concerns shifts from topic to topic (e.g., from the topic of violence in families to the topic of parents' responsibility toward kids). Although topic-to-topic shifts are possible, children tend to get bored with topical shifts and need more action in group work.

Holding the Focus

Children easily forget what the topic is, and if you aren't vigilant in holding the focus, they can change topics in the blink of an eye. They can also take the focus off an individual or an activity to meet their own needs. This is usually not done maliciously but because their minds wander and their needs for attention and affirmation are great.

Here are some examples of how to hold the focus, whether it be on a person, topic, or activity:

"We seem to be getting off the topic of what it means to be a friend. Let's get back to that now, OK?"

"I think we need to stay on the topic of how we deal with anger because there are lots of things we haven't said about it yet."

"Let's stay with Tyler a little longer and see if we can help him find some ways to talk to his stepdad in a respectful way to get his needs met."

"Luiz, you haven't had much air time today—let's stay with you a little longer and hear what you have to say."

"A lot of you seem to want to talk longer about breaking up with boyfriends/girlfriends. Let's stay on that topic for a few more minutes."

"Lanelle, we haven't finished our go-around yet, so we need for you to let the others have a turn talking about parents."

"I know that the topic of saying good-bye to our loved ones is painful to everyone, but we need to stay with it until we've heard from everyone."

"OK, let's stay on the topic of dating rights for now. We'll move on when everyone feels comfortable leaving this issue behind."

Whenever I think of or teach the skill of focusing I am reminded of the lyrics to a Kenny Rogers song "The Gambler": "You gotta know when to hold 'em, and know when to fold 'em, know when to walk away, and know when to run!" In the group you also need to know how to hold (stay on the topic), fold and walk away (leave a topic behind), and run (end the discussion and close the group). Being able to start, hold, and change the focus will help you feel much more comfortable about controlling what is happening and will help group members feel that you are in charge of the group's movement.

Resource

Jacobs, E. E., Harvill, R. L., & Masson, R. L. (1994). *Group counseling strategies and skills* (2nd ed.). Pacific Grove, CA: Brooks/Cole.

Practice: Focusing

The topic of discussion here is generally of interest to children at the upper elementary, middle school, or high school level. If you are working with younger children, you might try structuring an activity around the following types of topics: getting in fights in school, joining an after-school club, or playing a particular sport.

1. *Start the focus* by telling the group that the topic to be discussed is the benefits and risks of smoking. Let the group share some of their ideas on the topic for about 5 minutes.

2. *Shift the focus* from the topic to an activity by asking group members to list the benefits and risks they have been discussing on two sheets of newsprint that are hanging on the wall or a chalkboard. Give them about 10 minutes to finish this activity.

3. *Shift the focus* from activity to topic by asking group members to be seated in the group circle again to discuss their ideas and concerns.

4. *Hold the focus* on the topic for about 5 minutes or until group members have had a chance to discuss their ideas and concerns.

5. *Shift the focus* from a topic to the activity of processing. Ask the following questions:

> What did you learn from our discussion of the benefits and risks of smoking?
>
> What do you think you might do as a result of what you have learned?
>
> What did you learn about the other group members from this experience?

What was it like for you to share your values
and ideas about this topic?

6. Thank group members for their participation and end the
session.

THERAPEUTIC INTERACTION TECHNIQUES

Contracting

Overview

Contracting is a behavioral counseling technique with its roots early in the behavioral therapy literature. The technique has been described by such authors as Goodyear and Bradley (1980), Lazarus (1981), and Wysocki, Hall, Iwata, and Riordan (1979). Briefly, a contract is an agreement between the group leader and a group member concerning behavior. The leader can have similar contracts for behavior change with several or all of the group members or contracts specifying different target behaviors for different children, if that is the custom or purpose of the group.

There are two basic kinds of behavioral contracts: contingency contracts and informational treatment contracts. A contingency contract simply states that when a particular behavior is performed a specific reinforcement will occur, or if the behavior fails to occur a specific sanction will occur. An informational treatment contract is broader and includes (a) a description of strategies; (b) outcome goal expectations; (c) a client agreement to participate; (d) a statement of the time involved, such as number of sessions or days or weeks; and (e) some type of informed consent agreement (Seidner & Kirschenbaum, 1980).

Rationale

Contracts help the child follow through with and understand what will happen as a result of his or her behavior and clearly define the child as being responsible for behavior change. Contracts are very helpful with youths in groups because they state clearly what is expected and reduce the chance of game playing between counselor and group member by having every aspect of an agreement in the open. By giving children a clear understanding of what they need to do, contracts save time and energy. A special contract with each group member helps children individualize their behavior change plans. If appropriate, you can use the information from behavioral contracts to allow group members to experience how others in the group are progressing—this provides a model for success and perseverance.

The basic goals of using contracts in a group are the same as for contracts in individual counseling: to clarify each aspect of a behavior change plan and to ensure compliance. In using contracts in a group, an additional goal is to build a reinforcement networking system among the members so that they learn to receive feedback, support, encouragement, suggestions for improvement, and verbal rewards from their peers.

How to Use the Technique

A contract used with group members should include the following components:

1. A clear statement of the behavior to be increased, decreased, or eliminated. For example:

> Homework will be done four times per week.
>
> Desk will be straightened daily.
>
> Appropriate book and pencils will be taken to all classes.
>
> A certain number of library books will be read each week.
>
> No fights on the playground for one week.
>
> A certain number of positive assertions will be given.

2. Date the contract begins and date it is to be reviewed. For example, the contract could commence at the second group session and be reviewed weekly on Tuesdays.

3. Statement of the ways behavior is to change. For example, if the behavior is controlling anger to avoid fights, the contract might specify the following alternatives:

> Walk away from the situation.
>
> Count to 10 before I say anything.
>
> Think about the consequences.
>
> Tell an adult how angry I am and that I need a hug.

4. Persons involved in contract

5. Reward to be received for behavior

6. Bonus for extra positive behaviors

7. Penalty for negative behaviors

In using contracts in group work it is best to *keep it simple*, no matter what the age of the child. Figure 18 shows a sample contract that can be adapted to fit your situation. Complicated arrangements involving others outside the group or multiple problem areas are probably not suited to group work contracting. If you are using contracting with a single child as your client, you could involve two or three other adults—parent, teacher, and so forth—but if you are using a contract in a group, you will need to keep it between yourself and the child, or monitoring the contract will get out of hand.

In my opinion, group cohesion develops sooner when, if you choose to use contracts, they are used with all group members. Because they are all privy to the others' agreements, group members identify with one another in their change efforts.

Some additional suggestions for using contracts in a group are as follows:

1. Make copies of contracts that are easy for you and group members to fill in during a session.

2. Be sure you are able to deliver on any reinforcements. You might need to get in touch with parents to provide the particular reinforcement the child wants, at which point you would ask the child's permission to share the child's confidences with the parents. Kids usually are happy for their parents to have this information if they know it means they will get something neat!

3. Understand that if the child's teacher is involved with the contract, the child also needs to give permission because of the confidentiality rule for groups.

4. If the child's target behavior is so severe that it needs to be monitored daily, or more often than the group meets, it probably isn't a good choice for a group contract. You might need to work with this child individually until the behavior improves. Contracting works best with children who can self-monitor somewhat and don't need frequent contact.

5. Compliance is improved by clear understanding of the terms of the agreement. Be sure the child can articulate exactly what the contract says before you end the group session. If the child cannot repeat what he or she is supposed to do, compliance will be low.

6. Be sure to review the contracts frequently and give plenty of verbal reinforcement for children's efforts as well as for their accomplishments.

Most children enjoy using contracts because contracts allow them to receive feedback and attention not only from you but from other group members. Have the other children in the group applaud and praise the one sharing, and give treats or whatever has been decided on as a reward for the work. I find it helpful to have healthy snacks or treats on hand (raisins, crackers, etc.). You can give each child one treat for working on the behavior (effort) and two for full compliance. For example, if the child is working toward bringing in homework four times a week but has only brought it in twice, this is a step in the right direction. By rewarding small approximations of success, you give everyone a chance to succeed at something.

Resources

DeRisi, W. J., & Butz, G. (1975). *Writing behavioral contracts: A case simulation practice manual.* Champaign, IL: Research Press.

Goodyear, R. K., & Bradley, F. O. (1980). The helping process as contractual. *Personnel and Guidance Journal, 58,* 512–515.

Lazarus, A. A. (1981). *The practice of multimodal therapy.* New York: McGraw-Hill.

Seidner, M. L., & Kirschenbaum, D. S. (1980). Behavioral contracts: Effects of pretreatment information and intention statements. *Behavior Therapy, 11,* 689–698.

Wysocki, T., Hall, G., Iwata, B., & Riordan, M. (1979). Behavioral management of exercise: Contracting for aerobic points. *Journal of Applied Behavior Analysis, 12,* 55–64.

Practice: Contracting

Design and implement your own behavior contract for individual group members or for an entire group. The sample contract shown in Figure 18 is geared for the child from third grade up, and the behaviors listed pertain to the topic of anger management; adapt as necessary to your own situation.

FIGURE **18**

Behavior Contract

Name _____

Dates of contract: From _____ to _____

The angry behavior(s) I will work on is/are: _____

_____

The way(s) I am going to change my behaviors is/are:

_____ Count to 10 before saying anything.

_____ Decide just how angry I am about the situation
(low, medium, high).

_____ Think about consequences of my behavior.

_____ Walk away from the situation.

_____ Tell the person I am angry.

_____ Ask an adult to listen and give me a hug.

_____ Other _____

_____ Other _____

The person(s) I am going to practice controlling my anger with is/are:

_____

The reward I want to receive for controlling my anger is:

_____

The bonus I will receive for using _____ positive behaviors to
deal with anger in one day/week (circle) is:

_____

The penalty for using angry, hurtful behaviors is:

_____

Agreed to by _____ and _____

Date signed _____ Date reviewed _____

_____

Self-Improvement Homework

Overview

Group work with children is one means to help youngsters make significant changes in their lives. What happens during the session is part of the service, but equally important is what happens between sessions. If there is no transfer of learning to day-to-day life, then the group is essentially useless. Self-improvement homework can help accomplish this transfer.

Self-improvement homework is a behavioral assignment that the group leader and member agree will be practiced between sessions and reported on at the next session. It is usually a combination of cognitive, behavioral, and/or affective activities or exercises. For example, a cognitively oriented self-improvement exercise might be designed to reduce the number of negative self-statements a child makes. The child might be telling herself several times a day, "I can't do this," "I'm not smart," "I'm going to blow up and hurt somebody because I can't control myself," and so on. The homework might involve having the child monitor and write down what and how often she is saying these things. The next week the child could work on catching herself saying these things and replacing the negative statements with positive or coping statements. An affectively oriented homework assignment might involve a young child's working on making positive assertions of liking, loving, and affection—for example, saying something nice to a friend, his mother, or someone else twice a day. A behaviorally oriented homework assignment might be to complete academic homework twice that week and have it checked by a parent before handing it in to the teacher.

Rationale

Self-improvement homework has a purpose similar to that of academic homework: It extends the learning process beyond the instructional setting and provides the opportunity for realistic practice and reinforcement. Specifically, it encourages the transfer of learning to the child's everyday environment.

Specific goals of using this technique in group work are as follows:

1. To increase the children's sense of control of their behavior and responsibility for behavioral change

2. To shorten the amount of time it takes to make behavioral changes

3. To help children make decisions and connections about behavior that affects themselves and others

4. To engender a sense of universality (i.e., by suggesting that group members can work on problems and behaviors outside the group as well as in)

5. To increase the chances that children will reach their goals for being in the group

How to Use the Technique

During the process time of the group session, you can invite group members to participate in self-improvement homework related to the session or to their particular goals. This work needs to be voluntary; change cannot be mandated or legislated. For example, you can say, "Well, today we've role-played and practiced three ways to deal with anger situations. What would you be willing to do this week to try these ways out when you get in situations that push your anger buttons?" Usually one group member will offer to try them out; if not, you can directly ask who would be willing to practice them.

If you are going to use self-improvement homework, you will need to take the following steps if you expect the child to comply. Much frustration on your part, as well as frustration and feelings of guilt and lowered self-esteem on the part of the child, can be avoided by taking this responsibility.

Step 1: Provide a clear rationale. It is extremely important to give the child a clear and understandable *reason* to do the homework. If the child doesn't know why he or she is supposed to do the homework, compliance will be low. Be sure to ask the child to tell you why the homework is important. If the child can't repeat the reason in his or her own words, then the child probably doesn't know why and won't comply.

Not only does the child need to know why you think the homework is important, the child must also "buy in" to the reason. When explaining the reason for doing the homework, pay attention to the child's tone of voice and body language to ascertain whether or not you think the child understands the benefits. Ask yourself, "Would I do this if I were given the same instructions I have given this child?"

Step 2: Describe what to do. Clearly describe exactly what it is that needs to be done. The content of the homework comes directly from what happens in group; it needs to be something that the child has practiced and/or that you feel sure the child knows how to do.

Here are some examples of clear "what" statements:

Say positive things to friends or family, such as "I like you," "I appreciate you, Mom," "You look nice today," "I'm glad you are my friend," "I love you, Grandma," or "Thanks for helping me."

Do your homework (or chores, etc.) without complaining.

Leave the room when your brother starts an argument.

Ask your mom if you can do anything to help her.

Say, "Not in my gorgeous lungs" and walk away when someone offers you a smoke.

Say, "I can handle this" or "I can deal with this."

Listen to your relaxation audiotape.

Step 3: Specify how much or how often. Provide a clear statement of frequency so that the child knows how often to perform the behavior. Frequency should be the child's decision, not yours. The child is more likely to make a positive commitment to doing something he or she thinks is reasonable and is the best judge in this matter. Having the child determine and "own" this part of the input will enhance compliance.

Here are some examples of clear frequency statements:

Make positive statements to friends or family *two times each day.*

Do your homework (chores, etc.) *three nights this week* without complaining.

Leave the room *every time* your brother starts an argument.

Ask your mom if you can help her *once each day.*

Say, "I can handle this" or "I can deal with this"
five times each day.

Listen to your relaxation audiotape *once each day.*

Watch, listen, and help the child make a realistic commitment. Ask if anyone else could do something similar until all who want to have made a commitment. If a child seems to be excessive in making a commitment to a certain number of practices, help the child make a realistic commitment, regardless of what the other children are doing.

Step 4: Provide a way to record the assignment. Without some way to record the details of a homework assignment, after a day or two the child will forget how many times to do something and won't do it at all. So have self-improvement homework records like the example shown in Figure 19 available to fill out during the session and then take away. A good place for the child to keep this form is on a bedside table—before going to bed he or she can update it. (You may need to provide an envelope to keep the form in so the child can have some privacy from siblings who want to have a peek.)

Step 5: Remind the child to bring the record form to the next session. The homework record should include a reminder to bring the form to the next session. The child will see this reminder every time he or she uses the form but might also need some help from a parent to remember to bring the form on group day. Sometimes children enjoy working on their behavior and making changes by themselves and don't want to share this information with other family members. You can tell children that they can keep their work confidential and still ask a parent to help remind them to take the form on the right day. If you have already let the parents know that their child will probably be practicing certain behaviors and doing self-improvement homework, they will be better able to accept not knowing exactly what the child is practicing, thus preserving confidentiality.

Step 6: Process homework assignments and reinforce efforts. It is very important to process homework assignments if you give them. The following types of questions may help:

What did you learn about yourself by doing this homework/practice?

How did you feel after you completed it (satisfied, proud, relieved)?

What can you do now that you couldn't do before practicing?

What do you still need to practice?

Be sure to use the behavioral principle of reinforcing small approximations of success. However small the step a child takes each week, it is a step in the right direction, and you never know what impediments might have been overcome for that child to have made the effort. Be generous with praise and reinforcement!

You can choose to have some kind of external reward for homework practice or not, letting the praise and positive feedback from the group members serve as its own reward. (Small boxes of raisins or other healthy snacks are usually much appreciated.)

Finally, whenever you use self-improvement homework, you must ensure that the assignment reflects the child's needs. Each child has different coping skills, different stresses, a different tolerance for frustration, and a whole behavioral history that impinge on the situation. Making sure the assignment reflects individual needs does not necessarily mean you must create a different assignment for each group member, but self-improvement homework should always be flexible enough to allow a range of responses. For example, if the assignment is to practice assertion skills, you could give children the freedom to decide the person with whom they want to practice (mom, sister, friend).

Practice: Self-Improvement Homework

Identify a skill or behavior children could practice outside of the group session to reach group or personal goals. Adapt the form shown in Figure 19 as needed for your own situation. Item 5, "What I'm going to bring," is a prompt to help children remember to bring the form back to group session.

FIGURE **19** _____

Self-Improvement Homework Record

1. WHY (reason for doing homework)

_____

_____

_____

2. WHAT (what I'm going to practice)

_____

_____

_____

3. HOW MUCH (how much/how many times I will practice)

_____

_____

_____

4. RECORD (what I'm going to write down)

_____

_____

_____

5. BRING (what I'm going to bring)

_____

_____

_____

Feedback

Overview

Feedback is a mirror that allows group members to see how others experience them. Children and adolescents receive feedback regularly, whether they ask for it or not. Here are some examples:

Being chosen to be on a sports team indicates that one's athletic ability is valued; conversely, being rejected for the team gives the feedback that the youth is not "good enough" athletically.

Being elected to a class office gives feedback about popularity and leadership ability.

Getting a D in math gives the feedback that the teacher does not believe the child is achieving well in math during that period.

Having kids yell, "Get out of here, you sissy" gives feedback that the child is looked upon as a less than valuable play partner.

In the group situation, feedback means sharing information with another person about the effects of that person's behavior and having that person share the same kind of information with you. According to Kaul and Bednar (1978), feedback includes five dimensions:

1. Valence: Positive or negative nature of the message
2. Content: Behavioral aspect (describing behaviors) and emotional aspect (describing feelings of the person giving the feedback)
3. Source: Public or anonymous
4. Form of delivery: Written or spoken
5. Time reference: Here and now, or there and then

Rationale

In group work with adults, feedback has been considered a major factor in helping group members heal their psychological wounds

(Corey & Corey, 1992; Kaul & Bednar, 1978; Morran, Robison, & Stockton, 1985). In group work with children and adolescents, the purpose of feedback usually is to give members the information about themselves they need to modify behaviors that might be causing them problems in interpersonal relationships.

The specific goals of using feedback are as follows:

1. To help group members learn how they come across to others

2. To give and receive information that helps members learn more effective relationship skills

3. To allow all group members to have the chance to grow by making better decisions about being responsible for their own behavior

4. To give group members the opportunity to ask for and receive help, suggestions, and techniques to better meet their needs

How to Use the Technique

Feedback is a powerful technique and must be used cautiously. In using feedback in group work with youths, the first consideration is awareness of the level of group members' cognitive development. Children can learn to use feedback only if the concept is presented on their developmental level. The younger the child, the simpler and more concrete the feedback must be.

It is also important to keep in mind that group work with children is oriented toward social skill development, understanding and expressing feelings, and attitudinal change rather than insight. This is not to say that first or second graders cannot understand when someone else finds their behavior hurtful, but they are unlikely to change that behavior simply because they are given feedback. If Johnny punches Joey, Joey might say, "Ouch! That hurt me! Cut that out!" Although Johnny might stop punching, he would likely cease not because of the feedback that he is being hurtful but because he knows he will get in trouble.

Younger children are very self-oriented, and their thinking is concrete. Adolescents, on the other hand, are able to grasp what it means if their behavior bothers others, and if the information is shared in the right way and at the right time they can profit from direct verbal feedback. For example, if one group member comes in late for three sessions, another member might say, "Paul, when you come in late I feel mad because I had to hurry to get here on time, and you spent your time talking out in the hall and then get here late." When Paul hears how his dawdling in the hall affects others in the group, he can decide to change his behavior and get to group on time or go on doing the same thing. He knows how his behavior affects the others and that he is responsible either for making the change or for enduring the consequences of not making the change.

Teens often say, "So I do such and such—so what's the big deal?" They are not aware that their behavior really affects others. Peers react according to how another peer's behavior affects them. If the behavior is valued, peers respond in positive ways. When perceived as hurtful, the behavior is devalued and the response is negative. For example, 14-year-old Brett uses curse words continually, spits on the ground frequently, has dirty fingernails and hands, and wears a local gang's clothes, boots, and insignia. He acts "tough," making threats and pushing other kids around in the halls. Brett is trying to do whatever it takes to get accepted into the high school kids' motor gang. Some of the younger boys look up to Brett and think his behavior is "cool": It is valued and thought to be desirable. They give him feedback that he is valued by talking with him in the halls, giving him things, mimicking his behaviors, and wanting to be considered his friends. Another group of peers think Brett is bad news. They perceive his behavior as undesirable and certainly don't want to dress, act, or talk like him. He is devalued by them, and they give him feedback that he is undesirable by avoiding him, refusing dates, saying things like "You're weird," and valuing other things. When teens say, "What's the big deal? So I (drink, smoke pot, cut class, shoplift, drive recklessly)," the most useful feedback will come from their peers rather than you. As a result, it is important to have some youths in the group who have values and behaviors that can serve as models for others. If all of the youths are using alcohol, for example, they won't have the opportunity to hear the other side of the story or experience how their behavior comes across to these peers.

The research on feedback in groups gives us some specific ideas about how to use feedback in helpful ways:

1. Feedback should be about specific behaviors (not personality).

2. Positive feedback should be given first, then negative feedback.

3. Feedback exercises are best used later in the life of the group, in the working stage, and not earlier.

4. If the group is at the working stage and members are sharing both positive and negative feelings and behaviors, then honest and caring feedback has a good chance of helping members learn to build more effective relationships.

Both the research and my personal experience suggest that it is not a good idea to introduce structured feedback exercises or activities giving feedback, especially negative feedback, in the early stages of the group. You will need to have developed a working relationship with the group members, and the members with one another, before they will be open to feedback. One situation that does tend to occur spontaneously and frequently in the early life of a group concerns the monopolizing group member. When someone monopolizes intrusively, another group member will usually tell the monopolizer exactly what effect this behavior has: "Joni, you talk all the time and I never get my turn!" Clearly, you must deal with this member-to-member feedback immediately. However, structured feedback activities are better if left until later in the group process. If you are conducting short groups (say, six to eight sessions), there might not be much feedback given at all.

Modeling the delivery of feedback from the first session is very important because it sets the norm that group members are going to hear how what they do comes across. This prepares them to learn the skill of giving feedback to one another. For example:

"Debra, I really like the way you have been listening to everyone today. It shows you really care about people and that you're a good group member."

"Aaron, what a great job you did on the mural today! You did a super job with the drawings and gave other kids good ideas and feedback about their work so they could improve."

When giving negative feedback, try to be specific as to what behaviors cause a reaction; don't get hung up on describing personality traits. For example:

Don't say: "Lynn, you sure are mean."

Do say: "Lynn, when you keep on poking me and other kids in group I feel like poking you back. You could get our attention some other way."

206

Don't say: "Leigh is a slob."

Do say: "Leigh, when you come to group with your hair all messy, your hands dirty, and food from lunch on your face, it really turns me off. That's why I don't want to sit next to or talk with you."

The "Oreo cookie" method of giving feedback can be quite effective—that is, give positive feedback first, then negative, then positive. For example:

"Jill, I can see you have been trying very hard to keep focused on the topic of dating. Now you seem to be straying, so I wonder if you would go back to what girls think is most important in a relationship. I think you have some good insights on this."

"Leigh, you have been making a good effort to improve lately. I still feel put off when you come to group with messy hair and dirty hands. I know I would feel more friendly toward you if you'd clean up more often."

"Bobby, you make a lot less hurtful comments about people now. I like that. It really makes me mad to hear you say something about kids you don't even know. I hope you keep on being nicer to kids."

It is important to sit back sometimes and watch the traffic for a while to see what is happening before issuing negative feedback. If you miss dealing with a child who needs some feedback, most likely the behavior will occur again, and you will have another chance to intervene or have other group members intervene. Sometimes it is better that the behavior has occurred more than once; when the behavior reoccurs, the child can more readily accept the feedback. For example:

Leader to member: "Tiffany, I know you are trying to be a good group member. You have interrupted three times now, and I need for you to work on letting other kids have their turn. Can I count on you to work on that?"

Group member to member: "Rochelle, I hate it when you look off in space like you're brain dead every time I say something. I don't know what you're thinking about me, and I feel anxious. How about sharing what you're thinking?"

Group member to member: "Phillip, you say everyone picks on you and teases you. But you sit there and let them keep on and on after you, without saying anything to them or walking away. I don't feel sorry for you because you won't help yourself, and probably other kids feel the same way."

Resources

Corey, M. S., & Corey, G. (1992). *Groups: Process and practice* (4th ed.). Pacific Grove, CA: Brooks/Cole.

Hornibrook, L. K. (1995). *The effect of self-disclosure on the acceptance of corrective feedback in prepracticum training groups.* Unpublished doctoral dissertation, Indiana University Southeast, New Albany.

Jacobs, E. E., Harvill, R. L., & Masson, R.L. (1994). *Group counseling strategies and skills* (2nd ed.). Pacific Grove, CA: Brooks/Cole.

Kaul, T. J., & Bednar, R. L. (1978). Conceptualizing group research: A preliminary analysis. *Small Group Behavior, 9,* 173–191.

Morran, D. K., Robison, F. F., & Stockton, R. (1985). Feedback exchange in counseling groups: An analysis of message content and receiver acceptance as a function of leader versus member delivery, session, and valance. *Journal of Counseling Psychology, 32,* 57–67.

Practice: Feedback

Adapt the following feedback activities as appropriate for your group.

Animal-Animal

In a go-around, have each child name an animal that each other child reminds him or her of. For example: "Jesse reminds me of a bear because bears are soft and warm, and Jesse looks soft and warm" or "Carmel reminds me of a tiger because tigers walk up and down in their cages, and Carmel walks up and down in class and can't sit still." When everyone has had a turn, ask each child to give his or her reactions to what the others have said.

For older youths, use something other than animals—for example, trees or flowers (strong like an oak, shy like a violet), movie stars (loud like Madonna), foods (sweet like chocolate, tart like lemon), songs or poems ("You Are My Sunshine"), textures or colors (sandpaper, silk, chartreuse), or natural phenomena (mountain, glacier, pond, prairie).

Strengths Bombardment

In this exercise, all of the other members tell a designated member what they see as his or her strengths, while you or another group member writes them all down. The "bombarded" member can then keep the list to refer to and remember how others perceive him or her. If you determine that a certain member needs this feedback, you can conduct this exercise with just one member at a time. You can also conduct the exercise with each group member in a go-around. For example, you can say, "I wonder if we can give each person two or three strength feedbacks to take away today. Who would like to be first to hear what others think your strengths are?" Keep the go-around moving so that everyone gets a chance to hear some strengths.

My Wish for You

Corey et al. (1992) have suggested using the sentence stem "My wish for you is" to help group members give feedback in an acceptable way. The technique works well with youths from middle school age on up. For example, if a child has been struggling to learn new ways of dealing with anger, you could model and then ask the others to share:

> "Pablo, my wish for you is that you keep on trying to control your anger and eventually see that your work is worth the effort."

> "Pablo, my wish for you is that you see you can do it!"

> "Pablo, my wish for you is that you keep on taking a walk when you get mad like you did this week, because then nobody gets hurt."

> "Pablo, my wish for you is that your mom and dad see that you are really trying to be good."

Self-Feedback

Take a full-length mirror to group. Read the following poem aloud, then discuss:

> Just go to the mirror and look at yourself
> And see what the (boy/girl) has to say:
> For it isn't your father, or mother, or friend,
> Who judgment upon you must pass.
> The (boy/girl) whose verdict counts most in your life
> Is the one staring back from the glass.

Ask group members if they would be willing to take a look at themselves in the mirror, then identify and share one thing about themselves that they need to work on in relation to the topic of the group (e.g., to be a better friend to others, to control anger, to be more responsible, to understand divorce).

Structured Feedback

This activity is a good one to try in an ongoing group on the topic of friendship skills to give children insight into behaviors that are valued and not valued. It is effective with children from about fourth grade up, once the group is working well and the children trust one another.

1. In a go-around, have group members share something positive and negative about themselves as a friend. You might say, for example:

> We have been talking about friendship and friendship skills, and now it might be a good idea to take a good look at what we might be doing that makes us valuable as a friend and what we might be doing that could cause others not to like us. What I am asking you to do is for each person to share with us something about yourself that you and the others in the group believe is very precious and special about you as a friend and something that you have learned you need to work on because it causes others not to want you for a friend.

Sample responses include the following:

> Lenoir says, "The best thing I like about me as a friend is that I always stick up for my friends when someone else says something bad about them. The thing I need to do better at is not just talk to one friend so much but talk to all of them more."

> Jefferson says, "The best thing about me as a friend is I share my stuff with my friends. I'm not stingy. What I want to do better is not start fights with kids so I can get more friends."

> Patricia says, "I like it that I'm friends with a lot of kids, girls and boys, not just a few. I guess I need to work on not looking like I'm stuck up because I'm not, I'm just a little shy."

2. After everyone has had a turn, use the linking skill, described in Section 2, to have members connect about what they have to work on to improve their friendship skills.

Role-Playing

Overview

Role-playing has been described as "a situation in which an individual is asked to take a role (behave in a certain way) not normally his own, or if his own, in a place not normal for the enactment of the role" (Mann, 1956, p. 227). Quite simply, role-playing is trying out a new behavior for the purpose of experiencing what it is like.

Role-playing has been used by counseling and education professionals for decades to achieve both behavioral and attitudinal change. It is a component of the gestalt empty-chair technique, behavioral modeling, observational learning, and prosocial skills training, among other techniques. Videotaping and audiotaping are frequently used in role-playing to help children see their behavior as other children and adults see it.

Rationale

Role-playing as a technique in group counseling provides a model for improved behavior, the opportunity to practice in a safe environment, and positive reinforcement and feedback from peers to enhance behavior change. Most important, it allows children to see their own and other people's behavior from a new perspective. Research on learning through role-playing has demonstrated that we learn more readily and retain more by being active participants in the learning process; therefore, role-playing promotes learning more effectively than does observational learning alone (Iannotti, 1977; Mately & Acksen, 1976; Nichols, 1954).

Cognitive theorists such as Piaget indicate that during the preoperational stage, before the age of 11 or 12 years, children are unable to switch roles in their minds and understand how someone else is experiencing them. By acting out the role, it becomes more concrete. As a result, children gain insight and are motivated to change.

Some specific goals of role-playing are as follows:

1. To provide group members with a live learning experience to practice new behaviors

2. To allow children to participate actively in the attempt to change their own behavior

3. To allow group members to observe how their behavior affects others

4. To provide motivation, support, reinforcement, and feedback from peers to increase the chance that new behaviors will be learned

5. To allow group members to experience unfamiliar feelings, thoughts, and ideas

6. To encourage the development of new insights and behaviors through simulation of different roles

How to Use the Technique

Several kinds of role-playing exist, but the types most commonly used in group counseling with children are straight role-playing and role reversal.

Straight Role-Playing

In straight role-playing, the child plays the role of himself or herself, and the group leader and/or other group members play the parts of other persons in the situation. Straight role-plays are used if the child can benefit from being his or her own role model and does not need to see the behavior performed by someone else. The child must be old enough and bright enough to profit from this approach. If the child is very young or very insecure, he or she might benefit from first seeing other children act out the behavior, as in the participant modeling technique described next.

Some situations that would call for straight role-playing include the following:

Julie, an unassertive 9-year-old, wants to learn how to approach her teacher and ask him to explain the math lesson again.

Jorge wants to turn down cigarettes offered by other kids he hangs out with after school.

All of the group members want to learn how to ask a teacher to explain something about their grades on an assignment.

Some guidelines for using this type of role-playing are as follows:

1. In explaining what role-playing is, you might say that role-playing helps because it lets people practice before doing—just like practicing the piano before the big recital or rehearsing a speech before giving it in class.

2. If the role-play involves learning a behavior, you will need to have the group work together to break the skill down into steps to be learned. For example, if you are role-playing ways to respond to teasing, the group might decide the steps to follow are to stop and count to five, think about the choices (ignore the teasing, say how you feel, or give a reason for the person to stop), and act out the best choice (McGinnis & Goldstein, 1984).

3. If the situation is specific to one child in the group, it is best to coach the child to choose the other main actors in the role-play to be as much like the real-life people as possible.

4. To create distance, you can use puppets to play the parts of the people involved in the situation. (This is generally most effective with younger children.)

Role Reversal

In role reversal, the target person plays the part of someone else in his or her life and another child or the leader plays the part of the target person. Role reversal is a helpful technique when a child needs to understand another person's point of view.

Children often have a difficult time empathizing with how another person feels or thinks. Role-reversal is especially helpful in encouraging empathy in situations involving conflict—between child and parent, child and teacher or counselor, and child and peer. The goal of role reversal is to use the insight into someone else's point of view to make some behavioral or attitudinal change. The technique is also frequently used in career simulations to help young people find out what adult career roles are like.

The following situations might call for role reversal:

Kyle, age 8, hits smaller kids on the back when they are walking down the hall at school. He doesn't pick fights or get in trouble with older or bigger kids—just smaller or younger ones. He might be able to profit from learning what these kids think and feel when he hurts them.

Luisa and Maddy are very popular girls in sixth grade. They stand together in the hall and make hurtful and cutting remarks about the other girls' clothes, hair, boyfriends, makeup, where they live, whatever. Role reversal might help them experience the impact of their actions on these other girls.

The ninth graders in group are angry with Mrs. Washington for giving them extra homework because the whole class did poorly on a science exam. They think she is unfair and mean, and they want the group leader to go talk to her to convince her to rescind the homework. One of the group members could play the part of Mrs. Washington, who has spent a great deal of time preparing her students for the test, constructing the test, and now dealing with their anger.

Some specific guidelines for using role reversal include the following:

1. A good way of explaining role reversal is to say that it is like being in a play where you are someone else and someone else is you. The purpose of doing this is to find out how other people see you and what they think of what you do. You can also find out what it is like to be someone else.

2. Have the target child in a role reversal select the person who is going to play his or her part. The child selected should be similar to the target child in terms of sex, age, and background.

3. If the behavior of concern is physically hurtful, such as hitting or biting, instruct the child playing the target child not to hit or bite hard, that this is "acting" and the group can get the idea without anyone's really getting hurt!

Role-playing is a powerful technique, but it has its limitations: Some children are not cognitively ready to project themselves into the role of someone else. Such children are poor candidates for role-playing. Other children may be unable or unwilling to risk learning new behaviors in this way. Be sure a child is ready for this type of learning; too much pressure might discourage rather than reinforce the process of change.

Resources

Iannotti, R. J. (1977). Effect of role-taking experiences on role-taking empathy, altruism and aggression. *Developmental Psychology, 13,* 274–281.

Mann, J. H. (1956). Experimental evaluations of role-playing. *Psychological Bulletin, 53,* 227–234.

Mately, R. E., & Acksen, B. A. (1976). The effect of role playing discrepant positions on change in moral judgements and attitudes. *Journal of Genetic Psychology, 128,* 189–200.

McGinnis, E., & Goldstein, A. P. (1984). *Skillstreaming the elementary school child: A guide for teaching prosocial skills.* Champaign, IL: Research Press.

Nichols, H. (1954). Role-playing in primary grades. *Group Psychotherapy, 7,* 238–241.

Practice: Role-Playing

The following scenario illustrates how to use role-playing to help students ask a teacher to explain a grade on an assignment. Adapt as needed for your group.

1. Give group members a clear reason for doing the role-play. For example:

   Some of you have expressed a concern about how to approach a teacher with a question about grades. Today we are going to *role-play* a way you can ask this kind of question. Role-playing means pretending you are in a situation when you really aren't or taking on the part of someone else in a situation, like an actor in a play. Doing this can help you practice what you want to say and how the situation might go.

2. Have the group brainstorm what they should do before approaching the teacher—in other words, ask for an appointment or a time convenient for a private conversation, not just before a class when the teacher is busy.

3. Have the group brainstorm exactly what could be said. For example: "Mrs. Washington, would you please help me understand my grade on the science exam? I don't understand my scores on the questions."

4. Have the group brainstorm and write down a number of possible responses the teacher might give. For example:

   Latisha, each question is worth 5 points. You missed 5 questions, so you lost 25 points from 100 points. This equals your grade of 75 points.

   Latisha, let me reread your exam to see if I might have scored it incorrectly.

> Latisha, you didn't study enough—that's why
> you got a low grade.

> Latisha, you don't pay attention in class.

5. Pair the group members; ask one member to play the role of the student and the other to play the role of the teacher. Have each person playing the student use the same stimulus question, but have each person in the teacher role give a different response. Let the pairs work out how the conversation might proceed for a few minutes.

6. Reassemble the group, then encourage members to share how the dialogue went and how they handled the situation.

7. Process with the group what they learned from the experience and how they could improve on what they would say and do in a similar circumstance. Invite group members to practice their skills with a teacher if and when a situation like this arises.

Participant Modeling

Overview

Modeling, or the act of learning through observation, is one of the simplest yet most powerful and profound ways we have of knowing. Three specific types of modeling have been well-researched: The first is *symbolic modeling*, which involves the use of videotapes, audiotapes, slides, or films to present a model of the desired behavior. In the second type, *self as model*, the person records himself or herself on audiotape or videotape until an acceptable performance is achieved. (This technique is described next.) *Participant modeling* is the focus here. In this type, the person observes others performing the desired behavior in a setting such as a group, then practices each step of the behavior.

Developed by Albert Bandura (1976), participant modeling has been used with children and adults in a variety of situations to produce more effective coping and social skills. As a learning procedure, it has been researched heavily because of its importance in both school and clinical applications. Studies have shown that the technique can be successful in reducing child and adolescent fears and phobias (Davis, Rosenthal, & Kelley, 1981; Ladoucour, 1983), in social skills training with children (Gresham & Nagle, 1980), and in sexual abuse programs (Wurtele, Marro, & Miller-Perrin, 1987). The technique has also been applied with people who lack social communication and assertion skills. Generally, a model who has not completely learned the appropriate behavior, or a "coping model," is thought to be more effective in teaching a skill because, like the person who is learning, the coping model is still struggling to learn the behavior and is more realistic than someone who has perfected it (Bandura, 1976).

According to Bandura (1976) and Cormier and Cormier (1991), the steps in participant modeling are as follows:

1. Giving a rationale for using the technique

2. Dividing goal behaviors into subskills (which are easier and less threatening to master than the entire goal)

3. Instructing the client to note particular behaviors

4. Having models demonstrate as many times as needed

5. Having the client practice the demonstrated behaviors

I have adapted these steps for group work with children and adolescents in the following way:

1. Giving a rationale for using the technique

2. As a group, deciding on the subskill steps or better ways of dealing with the situation

3. Selecting group members or having group members volunteer to model the behavior

4. Having the members who have been selected or who have volunteered model the behavior for the target child

5. Having the target child practice the behavior and receive feedback from the group

Rationale

Participant modeling provides rapid reality testing because the behavior is practiced in the group, and group members give immediate feedback on progress. It is especially effective in reducing children's fears and helping them ask assertively for what they want or need, deal with social situations, and cope with performance anxiety.

The specific goals of using participant modeling are as follows:

1. To allow children to practice new behaviors and attitudes in the group and to encourage transfer of learning

2. To instill confidence in self to be able to master new behavior

3. To receive support and encouragement from others to practice the behavior

4. To practice in a safe, trusting environment before trying a new behavior outside the group

Some children take to this technique very readily, especially if they have some self-confidence to begin with and sufficient social skills to perform the behavior in the group. For children who are very shy and insecure, it might not be the technique of choice. Such children might respond better to watching others perform the behavior several times before trying it themselves.

How to Use the Technique

The following example shows how the steps in the participant modeling technique helped one child deal with other children who were teasing and harassing her on the bus.

Step 1: Give a rationale for using the technique. For example:

Annissa, you have said you want to work on getting the kids on the bus to quit teasing you. Maybe we can't get them to stop altogether, but we could practice some ways for you to deal with that situation right here in group so you could see and hear what to do. First, we would ask some group members to act out ways to deal with the teasers while you watch. Then you would act out the ways and see how it feels to deal with them yourself. After you practice here in group a few times, you might be ready to practice at home or even go ahead and do it when the situation happens again. What do you think? Would you be willing to try this kind of practice?

Note that in addition to explaining the rationale, the leader obtained the child's consent to try the technique.

Step 2: As a group, decide on subskill steps or better ways of dealing with the situation. In Annissa's situation, the group brainstormed the following alternatives:

Walk away or move to another place on the bus.

Ignore the teasing.

Start talking with a friend.

Tell the bus driver.

Tell the kids to stop teasing.

Tell the kids you feel hurt when they tease.

Tell yourself to calm down and count to 10.

Step 3: Select group members or have group members volunteer to model the behavior. In this situation, group members were eager to participate and several volunteered to take part in reenacting the situation.

Step 4: Have the members who have been selected or who have volunteered model the behavior for the target child. One group member played Annissa's part while two others took the role of teasers on the bus. The rest of the group took on a coaching role and whispered instructions and encouragement to the child playing the role of Annissa. The "real" Annissa observed the scene.

Step 5: Have the target child practice the behavior and receive feedback from the group. After the group role-played Annissa's situation, the leader asked Annissa if she felt ready to practice some of these ways, with the help of the rest of the group members. She consented, then played the role of herself in the same situation. After Annissa acted out the scene once, the group leader gave her positive feedback and praise for her efforts and asked the other group members for their feedback, too. The group then helped Annissa make some changes—specifically, using a more assertive tone of voice with the teasers and walking away with more conviction. The leader allowed Annissa to practice as many times as she needed to be comfortable with the new behaviors, asking her how she felt about each attempt. The group continued to provide encouragement and feedback.

In Anissa's case, the leader asked Annissa what she thought she would be willing and able to do as self-improvement homework before the next session (see the discussion of "Self-Improvement Homework" presented earlier in this section). Annissa decided that she would be able to ask her older sister in an assertive way to leave her belongings alone. At the next session, the leader followed up on Anissa's efforts to put the new behavior into practice.

It is important to give group members the opportunity to discuss their reactions to the participant modeling experience during the group's process time. Some helpful processing questions include the following:

(To the target child) What was it like to see other kids playing the role of you in the scene?

What did you learn from watching them?

(To the other role-players) What did you learn from playing the role of _____?

How did this help you?

(To the whole group) What do you think you will take away from this experience?

Finally, Corey and Corey (1992) remind us that being a model for our group members is one of the most important functions of group leadership. We can hardly expect to ask our group members to do something we are unwilling to model for them. Children especially need us to show them how to perform certain behaviors, such as using empathy statements, praising one another for progress, doing go-arounds, and processing each session. Each time you ask the children do to something new, model it for them if possible so that they can see exactly how it is done. They will learn so much more readily from watching a model of the behavior than by reading or hearing about it!

Resources

Bandura, A. (1976). Effecting change through participant modeling. In J. D. Krumboltz & C. E. Thoresen (Eds.), *Counseling methods* (pp. 248–265). New York: Holt, Rinehart and Winston.

Corey, G., Corey, M. S., Callanan, P., & Russell, J. M. (1992). *Group techniques* (4th ed.). Pacific Grove, CA: Brooks/Cole.

Corey, M. S., & Corey, G. (1992). *Groups: Process and practice.* (4th ed.). Pacific Grove, CA: Brooks/Cole.

Cormier, W. H., & Cormier, L. S. (1991). *Interviewing strategies for helpers* (3rd ed.). Pacific Grove, CA: Brooks/Cole.

Davis, A., Rosenthal, T. L., & Kelley, J. E. (1981). Actual fear cues, prompt therapy, and rationale enhance participant modeling with adolescents. *Behavior Therapy, 12,* 536–542.

Gresham, F., & Nagle, R. (1980). Social skills training with children: Responsiveness to modeling and coaching as a function of peer evaluation. *Journal of Consulting and Clinical Psychology, 48,* 718–729.

Jay, S. M., Elliott, C. H., Ozolins, M., Olson, R. A., & Pruitt, S. D. (1985). Behavioral management of children's distress during painful medical procedures. *Behaviour Research and Therapy, 23,* 513–520.

Ladoucour, R. (1983). Participant modeling with or without cognitive treatment for phobias. *Journal of Consulting and Clinical Psychology, 51*, 930–932.

Osborn, E. (1986). Effects of participant modeling and desensitization on childhood warm water phobia. *Journal of Behavior Therapy and Experimental Psychiatry, 17*, 117–119.

Perry, M. A., & Furukawa, M. J. (1980). Modeling methods. In F. H. Kanfer & A. P. Goldstein (Eds.), *Helping people change* (pp. 131–171). New York: Pergamon.

Russell, M. L. (1974). *The decision-making book for children*. Unpublished manuscript, Stanford University, Stanford, CA.

Wurtele, S., Marro, S., & Miller-Perrin, C. (1987). Practice makes perfect? The role of participant modeling in sexual abuse prevention programs. *Journal of Consulting and Clinical Psychology, 55*, 599–602.

Practice: Participant Modeling

Use the participant modeling technique to help a group member or members practice a new behavior. The steps are reproduced here to help you remember them; if desired, you can also help the child design and complete self-improvement homework.

Step 1

Give a rationale for using the technique.

Step 2

As a group, decide on the subskill steps or better ways of dealing with the situation.

Step 3

Select group members or have group members volunteer to model the behavior.

Step 4

Have the members who have been selected or who have volunteered model the behavior for the target child.

Step 5

Have the target child practice the behavior and receive feedback from the group.

Self as Model

Overview

In the self-as-model technique, developed by Hosford in the 1970s (Hosford, 1974, 1980; Hosford & de Visser, 1974), a child serves as his or her own model of a new behavior. The child practices a new and desired behavior that then is recorded on audio- or videotape. The child listens to or watches the tape, makes corrections in order to improve, and then rerecords until he or she is satisfied with the performance. The child then reviews the tape as necessary and practices the new behavior until it is acquired and put into use in everyday life.

The technique is a favorite of children and adolescents who are learning and practicing social skills and coping behaviors. The process I use, adapted from Cormier and Cormier's (1991) description of the self-as-model technique for adults, includes five steps:

1. Rationale for using the strategy

2. Recording the desired behavior

3. Making changes on the tape

4. Demonstrating the behavior on the tape

5. Homework practice with the corrected behavior on tape

The self-as-model approach works well with the following types of skills and/or behaviors:

Assertion skills, such as requesting help, giving opinions, asking for something, expressing negative emotions

Dealing with anger-provoking situations

Meeting new friends

Responding in class

Rationale

Why have children serve as their own models instead of having them watch another person performing the desired behavior, as in participant modeling, discussed previously? Research indicates that such model characteristics as age, sex, status in the peer group, and ethnicity have a positive influence on some clients and produce negative reactions in others (Bandura, 1971; Hosford, 1980; McDonald, 1973). As a result, some people respond better if they serve as their own model than if they watch someone to whom they might not be able to relate as well.

In addition, the self-as-model technique helps children build up their skills in a way that helps them feel self-confident. The use of the electronic equipment is highly motivating, and children strive to make corrections and get the feedback and praise of peers. The technique makes the behavioral performance more "real" and gives immediate, unquestionable feedback, thus enhancing accuracy in learning.

Specific goals include the following:

1. To teach a behavior the child wants to learn in a highly motivational format

2. To provide peer feedback and reinforcement for mastery of a desired behavior

3. To enhance transfer of learning

4. To avoid possible negative reactions associated with use of someone else as the model

How to Use the Technique

Each of the five steps in the procedure has a specific purpose, as shown in the following example.

Step 1: Explain the rationale for and give a brief description of the technique. Select a target child with whom to work. It is important to give a clear rationale for using the technique and briefly describe what will happen. Be sure you feel comfortable that the child is giving informed assent. You might say, for example:

> We have been talking about learning to be more assertive
> and getting our needs met. Several of you have mentioned

that it is hard for you to ask a teacher for extra help or to explain something again in class, yet you need to do this or your grades might be affected. I'd like to try a technique called "self as model," where you practice asking a teacher or someone else for something that you need in a positive, assertive voice, and we record your practice on this audiotape. Then we will play it back so you can listen to yourself. If you don't like how you sound, we'll erase it and start over until you feel comfortable with your use of assertive skills. Then you can take the tape home, listen to it, and perhaps go ahead and try the assertion skills in a real situation. Who would like to try it first?

Select one of the volunteers. Say, for example: "José, do you think this might help you reach your goal? Are you willing to try it with our help and coaching?"

Step 2: Have the group brainstorm suggestions for ways to perform the behavior. Record the child performing the behavior. With the target child, go over the behavior or behaviors to be learned. Write any instructions out on a chalkboard or flip chart for the entire group to see. Ask the rest of the group members if they have any suggestions. For example:

OK, José, now let's practice a little with the tape recorder because sometimes we aren't used to hearing our voices and it sounds strange. *(Spend a few minutes recording and erasing.)* What we'll do first is for you to decide what it is you want to ask your teacher about. Then I'll play the part of your teacher, and you'll play yourself. Say exactly what you would like, and we'll record it. Then we'll listen and you can tell us what you like and don't like about what you say. The rest of the group will then be your coaches and give you some help and suggestions for changes. What do you think? Are you ready?

Step 3: Have group members praise the attempt. Ask the target child to critique the performance; ask group members for ways the performance could be improved. Be sure to give lots of praise for the first attempt. Ask the target child what he or she liked about the performance, then ask the other group members what they liked (positive feedback only at this point). Then ask the child what he or she would like to change. After the response, ask the rest of the group for feedback on what the child could do to strengthen the performance. Rewind the tape to the beginning.

Step 4: Rerecord until the child is satisfied with the performance. Encourage the child to use the suggestions and record over the previous version. You might say, for example: "OK, José, go ahead when you're ready. I'll still be your teacher, and you be yourself. Change what you want to say however you think is best." Rerecord the message until the child feels comfortable that it is as good as it can be.

Step 5: Arrange for homework practice. Instruct the child to listen to the tape daily and practice it overtly or covertly, alone or with a friend or sibling. Have the child bring the tape back to group the next session and share with everyone the results of the practice. If things are going well, ask the child what he or she thinks the next homework assignment should be. Develop this next step with the child, being sure to go at his or her own pace.

This technique can be used in a group setting in a number of ways. As shown in the example, one child can be the target person, working on a particular skill, while the others serve as coaches and reinforce the behavior. Alternatively, small groups can work together. The small-group approach works well when several children are practicing a similar skill, such as a particular type of assertive response. You could divide a group of eight into two smaller groups. One child in each group would be working on a behavior change, while the other three would help by coaching and running the equipment. With adolescents I have had a group of eight divide into four pairs and go to separate places to audiotape verbal behaviors, such as practicing assertion skills, requesting help, and sharing opinions. If you are using a video set-up, only one child at a time should work on a behavior change; otherwise, it gets too noisy and confusing.

This technique is most effective if you have group members who are already working fairly well with one another and if the trust in the group is at least moderately high. It can be scary and unpleasant if the target child doesn't have enough self-confidence to work in front of the others or if the other children aren't able or willing to work as coaches and a support system for the target child.

Most children with adequate self-confidence will respond very quickly to being their own model—even acting a bit of a "ham" on tape—and will show positive results using the technique (Davis, 1979; Dowrick & Dove, 1980). However, children who are very shy and who do not have good self-esteem or social skills might be better served by watching someone else perform the behavior before practicing it for themselves.

One final concern: Be sure audio- or videotape equipment works before trying this technique with the group!

Resources

Bandura, A. (1971). Psychotherapy based on modeling principles. In A. E. Bergin & S. E. Garfield (Eds.), *Handbook of psychotherapy and behavior change: An empirical analysis* (pp. 653–708). New York: Wiley.

Cormier, W. H., & Cormier, L. S. (1991). *Interviewing strategies for helpers* (3rd ed.). Pacific Grove, CA: Brooks/Cole.

Davis, R. (1979). The impact of self-modeling on problem behaviors in school age children. *School Psychology Digest, 8*, 128–132.

Dowrick, P. W., & Dove, C. (1980). The use of self-modeling to improve the swimming performance of spina bifida children. *Journal of Applied Behavior Analysis, 13*, 51–56.

Hosford, R. E. (1974). *Counseling techniques: Self-as-a model film.* Washington, DC: American Personnel and Guidance Association.

Hosford, R. E. (1980). Self-as-a-model: A cognitive social learning technique. *Counseling Psychologist, 9*, 45–62.

Hosford, R. E., & de Visser, L. (1974). *Behavioral approaches to counseling: An introduction.* Washington, DC: American Personnel and Guidance Association.

McDonald, F. (1973). Behavior modification in teacher education. In *Behavior modification in education: 72nd yearbook of the National Society for the Study of Education.* University of Chicago Press.

Practice: Self as Model

> Use the self-as-model technique to help a group member or members practice a new behavior. The steps are reproduced here to help you remember them.

Step 1

Explain the rationale for and give a brief description of the technique. Select a target child with whom to work.

Step 2

Have the group brainstorm suggestions for ways to perform the behavior. Record the child performing the behavior.

Step 3

Have group members praise the attempt. Ask the target child to critique the performance; ask group members for ways the performance could be improved.

Step 4

Rerecord until the child is satisfied with the performance.

Step 5

Arrange for homework practice.

Responsibility Pie

Overview

To be responsible means to be held in account for or to be the cause of something. Several types of responsibility exist—for example, responsibility toward the self, responsibility toward others, moral responsibility, and legal responsibility. Although there are many opinions on how and what to teach in terms of responsibility, there appears to be agreement in the literature that children must be given the opportunity to learn responsible behaviors at an early age and that these efforts must be monitored and reinforced by significant adults throughout childhood and adolescence.

Parents, teachers, and adults in general are interested in children's learning and practicing responsible behaviors. At first glance, the concept of responsibility seems simple, but it is really quite abstract. How can an abstract concept be taught to children who think concretely? "Responsibility pie" is a technique I use in group work to help children and adolescents visualize and accept aspects of personal accountability for their behavior. In this technique, a circle (the "pie") represents 100% of the responsibility for any particular situation or behavior. The children are asked to accept *some* percentage of the responsibility, no matter how small. For example, a child may say, "Well, I'm only 5% responsible—my brother is responsible for the rest of it." The responsibility accepted becomes the basis for exploring what could have been done to avoid the problem and for behaving more responsibly in the future.

Rationale

Children dislike being blamed for things, either when they clearly understand that they are the cause or when they do not want to accept that they are the cause for fear of negative consequences. When someone points out lack of responsibility in a harsh way, children tend to blame someone else or find some reasonable explanation not to accept responsibility. For example, a parent might say, "Latonya, you left the peanut butter out on the front porch, and now there are bugs all over the jar." Latonya is likely to deflect the comment by saying, "But, Mom, I didn't know bugs would get into it!" In other words, she is not accepting personal responsibility for bugs ruining the food.

The responsibility pie technique helps children get the connection between the cause and effect of their actions in a nonthreatening, nonaccusatory way. It also helps them become part of the solution by teaching them to brainstorm better ways of dealing with problems. The process increases motivation to prevent situations from occurring that can be hurtful to themselves and other people.

Specific goals for using the technique include the following:

1. To explore the concept of responsibility and how it affects what children think and do

2. To help children learn that what they choose to do has an effect on others

3. To teach children that accepting responsibility for their actions can be a positive learning experience

4. To encourage understanding that responsible behavior results in positive feelings about self

How to Use the Technique

The practice section for this technique gives a step-by-step session plan for using the technique. The process follows the steps next described.

Step 1. Identify a situation in which a person did not behave responsibly. Clarify what was expected in the situation and what actually occurred.

Step 2. Draw a "responsibility pie" on a chalkboard or flip chart, then ask the group member or members to identify what amount of responsibility they are willing to accept. Draw lines on the pie to show the percentage of responsibility accepted. For example, if the child or children accept 20% of the responsibility, that percentage would look like the illustration on the next page:

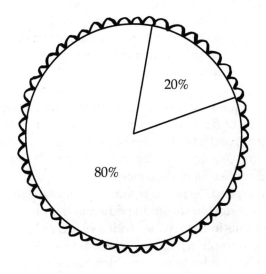

Redraw the piece below the pie, like so:

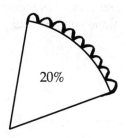

Step 3. Ask group members to suggest ways to be more responsible in that situation. In other words, no matter how much or how little responsibility the children are willing to assume, even if it is only 1%, ignore the percentage and use the fact that they accept any responsibility to help them explore better ways to accept ownership of their behavior.

The technique is best used with children who already have an understanding of fractions or percentages. Unless they are cognitively ready to handle the concept of percentages, the pie metaphor is not helpful. Usually children in the upper elementary grades and beyond relate well to the concept.

You can expand the pie metaphor by suggesting that sometimes our behavior results in something different than we had expected, just as ingredients in a pie change with cooking. For example, teasing someone could result in a fight where someone gets seriously hurt, or telling a young child to do something harmful in jest (e.g., "Why don't you go start a fire?") might result in the child's actually trying it and getting hurt.

It is important to use processing questions to help group members clarify and maximize what they have learned from the responsibility pie experience; the practice section includes some general processing questions you can use.

Practice: Responsibility Pie

Follow this procedure in an ongoing group to help members understand personal responsibility.

1. Draw a responsibility pie on the chalkboard or chart paper so the whole group can see it. While showing the picture, explain in developmentally appropriate language that the pie is a metaphor for a situation in which personal responsibility is involved. In other words, each person has a certain portion of responsibility in any situation.

2. Discuss one or both of the following situations, adapting as necessary for your own group.

Situation 1

Leland's responsibility at home is to keep his dog, Lad, fed, watered, walked, and played with every day. But Leland has been very busy with his friends for a couple days and hasn't walked Lad or played with him. Lad is full of energy and wants to get out and see what is going on in the neighborhood and have the kids play with him. Since he hasn't been walked or played with, Lad gets bored and begins to chew his rope. He chews it until it breaks through and then runs off to explore and play! That night Leland goes out to feed and water Lad but finds the dog's rope chewed and no dog. Leland is very upset and feels terrible that he hasn't taken good care of Lad. But he doesn't want to accept responsibility for his poor care of Lad and tells his family that it is Lad's fault—he wouldn't stay home and be a good dog.

Ask the following questions:

What part of the responsibility pie belongs to Leland?

What part of the responsibility pie belongs to Lad?

What part of the responsibility pie belongs to others?

Let the children say how much responsibility Leland has for the situation. Take a marker and draw a piece on the responsibility pie representing approximately what percentage belongs to Leland. For example, suppose the children determine that Leland has about 20% of the responsibility. Mark out about one-fifth of the pie as if you were going to cut a piece that size. Redraw the piece below the pie. Say to the group, "If this is about how much responsibility Leland has for Lad, what could he have done differently to be more responsible and prevent the dog from running away?" For example:

He could have taken Lad with him when he went with his friends.

He could have asked his sister if she would walk Lad in exchange for his doing one of her chores for the day or the weekend.

He could have told his friends he couldn't be with them until he took care of his responsibility for Lad.

He could have told his parents that he was extra busy and asked them what they thought he could or should do.

Situation 2

It is July, and Paul just turned 16 and got his driver's license. He is excited about being able to go places on his own and with his friends. His sister, Cathy, works at the bank, and her car is at Bergin's Auto Repair being fixed. Paul has agreed to pick up Cathy after work at 5:00 P.M. and bring her home because she has health problems and can't wait for long outside in the hot sunshine. Paul's friends ask him to take them to get milkshakes after school because it has been over 100 degrees that day. They keep clowning around, goofing off, and the time gets later and later. Pretty soon it is 5:00 P.M., and Paul is supposed to be a half-hour away at the bank picking up Cathy. His friends tell him not to worry—his sister is OK and

240

can take care of herself because she is 19 and doesn't need her 16-year-old brother watching over her. Paul is getting more and more anxious because he promised Cathy he'd be there right at 5:00, and now he can't get rid of his friends.

When he finally gets to the bank to pick up Cathy, there are several police cars around and an ambulance out front. Paul is panicky and asks the officer who stops his car what happened. The officer says a young woman fainted in front of the bank and is being taken to the hospital. Paul tells the officer that it might be his sister and is taken to the ambulance to see. It is Cathy; even though she is feeling much better, they take her to the hospital anyway. Paul goes home to the family, who have already been notified by the police. Paul feels absolutely horrible because he thinks that if he had been there for Cathy she might not have gotten overheated and passed out.

Ask the following questions:

Out of 100% of the responsibility for this situation, how much is Paul's responsibility?

How much is Cathy's responsibility?

Who else has responsibility?

Suppose the children say that 60% of the responsibility is Cathy's because she is older and should know how to avoid health risks. That would leave 40% of the responsibility as Paul's, for giving his word he would be there on time. Draw a piece of the pie to show 40% as Paul's responsibility. Redraw the pie piece below, then ask what Paul could have done to be more responsible. For example:

He could have refused to take his friends to get milkshakes if he thought he might be late.

He could have left his friends at the burger place and gone to pick up Cathy.

He could have taken his friends with him so he wouldn't be late.

3. Ask the children in the group if they have a situation of their own they would be willing to share, then go through the process for that situation. Sometimes children will use a friend's or sibling's indiscretion rather than their own, but as they begin to trust, a group member will usually self-disclose.

4. Process the experience, using the following kinds of questions:

What did you learn about accepting part or all of the responsibility for doing something?

At what age are children responsible for things they say they are going to do?

What should you do if you find out that you can't follow through with something you accepted responsibility for?

What should you do if you behave irresponsibly and someone or something gets hurt?

Progressive Muscle Relaxation Training

Overview

Most adults are aware of how much stress, tension, and anxiety is a part of everyday life. We usually are not as aware of the amount of stress children and adolescents experience, and their natural vivacity and high energy level often mask how stress drains their physical and mental resources. Many children are up and waiting for the school bus at 6:30 or 7:00 A.M. and return late in the afternoon after extracurricular activities or being taken care of at a sitter's until a parent picks them up after work. They have academic and emotional demands we didn't face as children when we were growing up.

Early research on stress focused on defining what stress is and how it affects our performance (e.g., Jacobson, 1929; Lazarus, Deese, & Osler, 1952). In the 1970s and 1980s, research on techniques to deal with excess stress emerged in medicine, psychiatry, education, and various applied mental health fields (e.g., Benson, 1976; Denniston & McWilliams, 1975; Lehrer & Woolfolk, 1982). Four therapeutic approaches have emerged as ways to cope with, eliminate, control, or avoid stress responses. These include cognitive, behavioral, environmental, and physiological techniques (Budzynski & Peffer, 1980).

Relaxation skills can help children deal with anticipated stressors (e.g., taking an exam or going to the dentist) or relax after stressful situations (e.g., having an argument with a friend or getting a bad grade on a test). Sometimes relaxation skills are taught as stand-alone techniques, and sometimes relaxation is part of another technique, such as in stress inoculation, covert modeling, or systematic desensitization.

I have used the physiological technique of progressive muscle relaxation training, as described by Cautela and Groden (1978), with good results in groups of children and adolescents, and this type of relaxation training is the focus here. In general, the procedure involves a four-step process of tensing muscles, noticing how the muscles feel when tense, relaxing the muscles, and noticing how the muscles feel when relaxed. The process is repeated through the major muscle groups of the body, resulting in an all-over feeling of relaxation.

Rationale

Children and adolescents who find themselves in a group counseling situation are usually those who need additional help in learning social and coping skills; frequently, they experience a great deal of stress because of psychological and/or educational deficits. Progressive muscle relaxation gives children a technique or tool they can use wherever they are, in whatever situation causes them distress, for the rest of their lives. Unlike some counseling techniques, which are limited in usefulness to clients of at least average intelligence and a certain degree of cognitive maturity, this technique can be used with nearly all intellectual levels and ages. It is extremely versatile and takes only limited practice to master. It can be taught to children with special education and physical needs, provided the cautions noted are observed.

Specific goals of the technique are as follows:

1. To help children identify stress in the form of muscular tension and be able to lessen the effects of the stress by relaxing the muscles

2. To help children learn a skill that can be used before, during, or after stressful situations to lessen the effects of stress and anxiety

How to Use the Technique

Relaxation skills can be taught during a group counseling experience and then applied to stressful situations related to any group topic: divorce, loss, anger management, school survival, and so forth. The skills can be taught to the group as a whole and practiced individually between sessions.

The practice section for this technique provides a progressive muscle relaxation script that can be followed in the group session. Before using this script, please be aware of the following cautions and considerations:

1. Do not use the exercises with children who have medical problems that might be affected by the tightening of the muscles during the tensing phase. Children with multiple sclerosis, arthritis, heart or blood pressure problems, asthma, or muscle problems are at risk. If there is any doubt, be sure to ask the child's parents and get medical clearance.

2. Stress that the relaxation exercises are a skill, and like any other skill (playing the piano, basketball, etc.) children will need to practice every day to learn how to do them correctly.

3. Have the children talk about what time of day and where they can practice without being disturbed. If they have siblings who are teasing or bothering them, they won't be as likely to practice, and the learning process will take longer. They will need to determine a regular schedule for practice, such as a half-hour before bedtime.

4. Because it is hard to remember all of the body parts to tense and relax, having the parts listed on a page to take home is helpful. Other options include giving the child an audiotape of the session or having a parent help the child practice.

5. Some children are embarrassed about doing the tensing and relaxing exercises and need help and encouragement in knowing what to do. (Adolescents especially feel strange if they don't look glamorous in front of their peers.) Assure them that it is OK to be self-conscious and that everyone is too busy tensing and relaxing his or her own muscles to be watching anyone else.

Resources

Benson, H. (1974). Your innate asset for combating stress. *Harvard Business Review, 52*, 49–60.

Benson, H. (1976). *The relaxation response*. New York: Avon.

Budzynski, T., & Peffer, K. (1980). Biofeedback training. In I. Kutash & L. Schlesinger (Eds.), *Handbook on stress and anxiety* (pp. 144–158). San Francisco: Jossey-Bass.

Cautela, J. R., & Groden, J. (1978). *Relaxation: A comprehensive manual for adults, children, and children with special needs*. Champaign, IL: Research Press.

Denniston, D., & McWilliams, P. (1975). *The TM book*. New York: Warner.

Jacobson, E. (1929). *Progressive relaxation*. The University of Chicago Press.

Lazarus, R., Deese, J., & Osler, S. (1952). The effects of psychological stress upon performance. *Psychological Bulletin, 49*, 293–317.

Lehrer, P., & Woolfolk, R. (1982). Self-report assessment of anxiety: Somatic, cognitive, and behavioral modalities. *Behavioral Assessment, 4*, 167–177.

Practice: Progressive Muscle Relaxation Training

Explain the rationale for using progressive muscle relaxation. Have group members wear comfortable clothes and sit in chairs with plenty of space between them. Darken the room a little, then read the following script in a slow, calm voice. Walk around to help any children who need assistance in getting the sequence right.

When you feel tense, upset, or nervous, certain muscles in your body tighten. By having you deliberately tense certain muscles in your body, you will learn to identify the muscles that are tight; then you learn to relax them. Practice tightening and relaxing the following muscle groups.

Forehead

Wrinkle up your forehead. Point to where it feels particularly tense (over the bridge of the nose and above each eyebrow). Slowly relax your forehead and pay special attention to those areas that are particularly tense. Spend a few seconds noticing how it feels to have those muscles loosen, switch off, and relax. Notice the difference in how the muscles feel.

Note. From *Relaxation: A Comprehensive Manual for Adults, Children, and Children with Special Needs* (pp. 22–30) by J. R. Cautela and J. Groden, 1978, Champaign, IL: Research Press. Copyright 1978 by the authors. Reprinted by permission.

Eyes

Close your eyes very tightly. Point to where it feels tight. Your eyes should feel tense above and below each eyelid and on the inner and outer edges of the eye. Pay particular attention to those areas that are especially tense. Gradually relax your eyes as you open them slowly. Notice the difference in the way the muscles feel.

Nose

Wrinkle your nose. Point to the areas that feel tight (the bridge and nostrils). Pay special attention to those areas that are particularly tense. Gradually relax your nose slowly, letting all the tension out. Notice how it feels to have those muscles loosen, switch off, then fully relax. Notice the difference in the way the muscles feel.

Smile

Put your mouth and face in a forced smile. Point to the areas that feel tense (the upper and lower lips and cheek on each side). Your lips should be hard against your cheeks. Gradually relax your face. Notice how it feels to have those muscles loosen, switch off, and relax.

Tongue

Put your tongue hard against the roof of your mouth. Point to where it feels tense (on the inside of the mouth and tongue, and the muscles just below the jaw). Slowly relax those muscles by letting your tongue gradually fall to the floor of your mouth. Pay special attention to those areas that are particularly tense. Notice how it feels to have those muscles loosen, switch off, and relax. Notice the difference in the way the muscles feel.

Jaw

Clench your teeth. Point to where it feels tense (the muscles on the side of your face and also the temples). Gradually relax your jaw and feel the sensation of letting go. Notice how it feels to have those muscles loosen, switch off, and relax. Notice the difference in the way the muscles feel.

Lips

Pucker your lips. Point to where it feels tense (upper and lower lips and side of lips). Pay special attention to those areas that are particularly tense. Gradually relax your lips. Notice how it feels to have those muscles loosen, switch off, and relax. Notice the difference in the way the muscles feel.

Neck

Tighten your neck. Point to where it feels tense (Adam's apple and on each side and the back of the neck). Pay special attention to those areas that are particularly tense. Gradually relax your neck. Notice how it feels to have those muscles loosen, switch off, and relax. Notice the difference in the way the muscles feel.

Arms

Put your right arm out straight, make a fist, and tighten your whole arm from your hand to your shoulder. Point to where it feels tense (biceps, forearm, back of arm, elbow, above and below wrist and fingers). Pay special attention to those areas that are particularly tense. Gradually relax and lower your arm, bending it at the elbow; relax so that your arm is resting on your lap in the relaxing position. Notice how it feels to have those muscles loosen, switch off, and relax. Notice the difference in the way the muscles feel. Repeat with the left arm.

Legs

Now lift your left leg, turn your toes in towards you, and tighten your whole leg. Point to where it feels tight (top and bottom sides of thigh, knee, calf, front and back of arch, and toes). Gradually relax and lower your leg until your foot is squarely on the floor, bending your knee as you relax. Make sure your leg goes back to the relaxing position. Notice the difference in the way the muscles feel. Repeat with the right leg.

Back

Move forward in your chair. Bring your elbows up and try to get them to meet in the back. Notice where it feels particularly tense (shoulders and down the middle of your back). Gradually relax by moving back into the chair while you straighten out your arms and put them on your lap in the relaxing position. Notice how it feels to have those muscles loosen, switch off, and relax.

Chest

Tighten your chest. Try to constrict it or pull it in. Point to where it feels tense (middle of the chest and above and below each breast). Gradually relax your chest. Notice how it feels to have those muscles loosen, switch off, and relax. Notice the difference in the way the muscles feel.

Stomach

Tighten your stomach by pulling it in and making it as hard as a board. Point to where it feels tense (navel and circle around navel encompassing about 4 inches in diameter). Gradually relax your stomach to its natural position. Notice how it feels to have those muscles loosen, switch off, and relax. Notice the difference in the way the muscles feel.

Below the Waist

Tighten everything below the waist, including your thighs and your buttocks. You should feel yourself rise from the chair. You may notice that you have to tighten your legs a bit. Notice where it is particularly tense (top, bottom, and sides of thighs; muscles from the rear that make contact with the chair). Gradually relax and move back in your chair. Notice the difference in the way the muscles feel.

"I" Statements

Overview

A significant communication skill in interpersonal relationships is immediacy. Immediacy means to be able to describe thoughts, feelings, or behaviors at a particular moment, as they are happening. We frequently go for long periods not being self-aware until some event occurs that impinges on our consciousness. For example, you might not be aware that the muscles in your neck are tense. Suddenly, after a couple hours sitting at a desk or in front of a computer screen, you realize that your neck is sore and that you need to move around or do some relaxation exercises. The same type of insensitivity to what is happening at the moment is true in relationships. Generally, we have been taught to disregard our feelings, especially anger and irritation, and sometimes we "stuff" these feelings rather than say something about them when they occur.

Making thoughts and feelings immediate can bring us into the "here and now" and help us be more real. One way to be more immediate in relationships is to use "I" statements, also called "I" messages. An "I" statement is a communication that states how an individual is feeling, what behavior is involved, and what the individual would like to have done about the situation. One "I" statement formula is as follows:

I feel _____ (emotion)

when _____ (behavior occurs),

and I need/would like _____ (what you would like to have happen.

This simple formula helps the individual take ownership of and responsibility for his or her own feelings and express them in the moment. In this context, "taking ownership" means accepting the feelings or thoughts as one's own, not caused by someone else.

"I" messages let another person know your feelings or thoughts on an issue and communicate that you take ownership of your feelings. They also convey that you are upset in some way and that you would like to have the person behave in a different way.

251

Because they do not blame or discredit the person receiving them, "I" messages increase the chance that the other person will listen and want to make a positive response.

The opposite of "I" messages are "you" messages. When we experience negative emotions, we tend to blame someone else for that feeling or situation. For example:

"You left the back door open and let that bee in!"

"You are so dense! You never remember to put your bike away."

"You forgot to do your homework again?"

"You never clean up after yourself!"

When we use "you" statements, the other person hears the statement as blaming and as a result feels guilt, hurt, aggravation, or other negative feelings. "You" statements usually result in the person's shutting down to your requests, not opening up to you. Your intent might be to have the other person change a behavior, but the chances are that once the person hears a "you" statement, he or she is no longer listening.

Rationale

The purpose of using "I" statements is to accept personal responsibility for one's own thoughts and feelings in the immediacy of the moment, to communicate those thoughts and feelings to another person so that person is aware of them, to let the person know you want some behavioral change, and to remain open to discussing how things can improve.

In brief, teaching "I" statements in group helps children learn responsible acceptance of their own feelings and how to communicate in a respectful way so that others are more likely to understand and comply with their requests.

How to Use the Technique

"I" statements are a natural way to express the feelings that will come up in topical groups focusing on such issues as assertion skills, self-esteem, anger management, relationships/friendships, getting along with parents and teachers, divorce, and death. If you teach the "I" statement formula early on in the life of the group, children can use the formula as the need arises. They learn quickly because they are reinforced by their peers. Once the children are somewhat secure about being assertive, you can encourage their use of "I" messages with people outside the group.

Because "I" statements may be a much more assertive way of communicating than the children have used before, try to get a sense of how parents might react before recommending that they practice at home. Some parents might be offended by what you would consider appropriate assertion, and the technique might not be right for their children.

Resource

Cormier, W. H., & Cormier, L. S. (1991). *Interviewing strategies for helpers* (3rd ed.). Pacific Grove, CA: Brooks/Cole.

Practice: "I" Statements

Follow this procedure to help group members learn to
construct "I" statements. Be sure to model and point out
the use of "I" statements as the group continues.

1. Explain to group members that when we are angry or hurt by
   someone, we often communicate in such a way as to make them
   feel blamed or responsible for our feelings. We are responsible
   for our feelings, not someone else. Often we use "you" messages,
   such as "You make me mad when you are always late" or "You
   shouldn't leave my VCR on when you are finished with a movie."
   The person gets the message that you are unhappy, but instead
   of being motivated to change, the "you" message leaves the
   person feeling hurt or angry.

2. Ask group members how they would react to the following
   statements:

   > "You left the refrigerator door open again!"

   > "You didn't take the newspapers out to be recycled!"

   > "You haven't fed the dog yet?"

   > "You didn't do your homework again?"

   > "Your room is a mess! You never clean it right!"

3. Explain the rationale for using "I" statements as being to have a
   way to express our negative thoughts and feelings to other people in a way that helps them listen and want to comply. Explain
   that "I" statements are used when we want to communicate
   negative feelings to someone and we would like them to make
   a change in their behavior.

4. Write the "I" statement formula on a chalkboard or flip chart:

> I feel _____
>
> when _____ ,
>
> and I need/would like _____ .

For example:

> "I get aggravated when you leave soda cans and pizza crusts in your room, and I want you to clean up after yourself every night before bed."
>
> "Mommy gets upset when you leave your jammies on the floor, and I want you to hang them on the hook when you take them off."
>
> "I feel worried when you don't come home at the agreed upon time, and I want you to either be home or call and let me know where you are."

5. Ask for situations when the children felt angry, upset, scared, or whatever and model use of the formula. Stress that using "I" statements instead of "you" statements to communicate our feelings to others respects both our needs and the others' feelings.

6. After you have modeled the use of "I" statements, give members a copy of the situations listed in Figure 20 (adapt as needed to suit your own group). Help group members use the formula to create "I" statements for the first four or five situations, then divide into dyads and have them write their own "I" statements for the rest of the situations.

7. If time permits, dyads can also create "I" statements for situations of their own, or group members could role-play the use of "I" statements in situations that come up with their friends, family, or people at school.

FIGURE **20** _____

"I" Statement Situations

Situation 1

Your brother borrowed your favorite shirt and tore a hole in it before putting it back on your bed. What do you say to your brother?

Situation 2

Your teacher thinks you copied someone else's paper and gave you an F. What do you say to your teacher?

Situation 3

Your dad, who lives 40 miles away, did not come to pick you up for your Saturday visit with him. What do you say to your dad?

Situation 4

Your best friend asked your girlfriend/boyfriend out on a date. What do you say to your friend?

Situation 5

Your mom has promised to give you some money three times, and now she says you can't have it. What do you say to your mom?

Situation 6

The coach said you aren't working hard enough to stay on the team. What do you say to your coach?

Situation 7

The band teacher thought you were at fault for leaving the band room a mess and gave you a detention. What do you say to your band teacher?

Situation 8

Your little sister took your best notebook and tore all the pages out. Yesterday she drew on your math book. What do you say to your little sister?

Situation 9

A kid in your neighborhood poked a hole in your basketball. What do you say to the kid?

Situation 10

Your science grade is D. Your teacher won't give you more time to finish your science project, which is due tomorrow. What do you say to your science teacher?

Situation 11

Your older brother always gets home from school first and eats all of the snacks that your mom leaves out for the both of you. What do you say to your older brother?

Situation 12

You gave up going to a show with friends to help another friend study for a test. You waited at the library for 2 hours, and the friend never showed up. You missed the show and still didn't get to study. What do you say to your friend?

Closing Rituals

Overview

The first session of a group is critically important in establishing norms, beginning to get members comfortable and connected, and developing a pattern for what is to come. The last session is also important because it presents a special opportunity to review what the members have learned, revisit some of the joys and pains of the group, and make plans to keep on working on behavior changes in the future. Children frequently become very attached to their group. Sometimes it is the only place where they are listened to, valued, and encouraged, so giving up the group can be a crushing loss. Closing rituals can help during this time.

A ritual is a ceremony or a series of actions that is followed regularly. When a group counseling experience is over, certain group work tasks need to be accomplished. Children and adolescents love parties, gifts, and sharing special foods (pizza, cake, etc.). A closing ritual for children, then, combines the tasks that are regularly included in ending a group, plus some activity or goodies that the children can enjoy and remember as part of their learning experience. It is a planned experience for the final session of a group that helps the leader and members consolidate learning and say good-bye to each other in a healthy way.

Rationale

Frequently, children experience trauma when emotional relationships end. For example, a parent may suddenly move out, a grandparent may have an unexpected heart attack and die, or an older brother or sister may leave to get married or go to college. Significant people in children's lives are suddenly not there, and there is no time to say good-bye or get some kind of closure. Adolescents experience intense boy/girl relationships of varying durations, then break up. Breaking up is part of the natural learning process adolescents are going through, but many times one partner breaks the relationship off without explanation. This type of "dumping" results in great pain and misunderstanding.

259

Ending relationships is difficult at best, and in our society most of us lack the coping skills to deal with loss in a growth-promoting way. Closing rituals help children transition out of the experience without feeling "dumped" or abandoned. By creating a special, memorable ritual to end the group, you are in a small way suggesting a more positive, less hurtful way for children to deal with future endings in their lives.

The specific goals of using a closing ritual in a group are as follows:

1. To review and consolidate what has been learned in the group

2. To provide an opportunity for feedback to other group members

3. To clarify what needs to be worked on in the future

4. To model a way to get closure in relationships and to suggest that ending is a natural part of relationships

5. To have an enjoyable time together to celebrate the learning experience

How to Use the Technique

The last session of a group should include the following components:

1. A reminder to keep the information shared in the group confidential, even after the group is over

2. Systematic processing of the learning experiences of each session. You can do this by briefly describing each session and asking children what they remember about or learned from that session. If the group was very long and/or there were no specific topics, you could ask children to identify the three most important or valuable things they learned.

3. Processing of the overall group experience, using questions such as the following:

> What is the most important thing you learned during this group?
>
> What do you still need to work on?
>
> What did you learn that you are the most proud of?
>
> What are you disappointed in about the group?
>
> What did you learn about yourself?

What did you learn about the topic of the group?

In what ways do you feel better now?

In what ways do you feel worse now?

How are you going to use what you have learned?

4. A special activity or treat

With older children, you could add to this list asking each child to share something positive he or she learned from each other group member. This takes a while, so if you choose to do this, allow enough time for everyone to have a chance to share.

It is very important to remind group members in advance that the group will be ending at the designated time. If the group is a 10-session topic-oriented group, you would want to remind them on the eighth session that there will be only two more sessions. On the ninth session, you would remind them again that the next session will be their last and that the group won't be together again in the same way, so they will be saying good-bye. If the group is devoted to long-term therapy, you will need to begin winding down even earlier and perhaps taking more than one session for the closing ritual. Reminders have a twofold purpose. First, if members have things they want to talk about in group, they will know that the time is limited and they need to get busy and bring these issues up. Second, members will be able to seek out more help or counseling if they know the group support system will no longer be there in the same form.

Before the last session, you can also ask the children what they would like to do to end the group experience. Because their experience is limited, they usually say "a party," which can be renamed "a celebration of us" or something else appropriate.

Resource

Cormier, W. H., & Cormier, L. S. (1991). *Interviewing strategies for helpers* (3rd ed.). Pacific Grove, CA: Brooks/Cole.

Practice: Closing Rituals

> Use one of these activities at the end of the last group session
> to help children celebrate the group experience. Adapt to
> suit to the developmental level of group members and/or
> the group topic.

"Warm Fuzzy" Bags

Give group members a brown paper lunch bag and crayons or
marking pens. Each member will also need a strip of paper for
each other group member, including yourself. Have the children
write their names on the front of their lunch bags, then write a
"warm fuzzy" statement about each other child in the group on
the strips of paper. For example:

> "Kristin, thank you for helping me learn to be a better
> friend. You are about the best kind of friend a kid could
> have."

> "Fred, you helped me a lot. You have a big heart and
> helped us all. Thank you."

> "Matt, I like the way you say what you feel right out.
> I want to learn to be more like you."

> "Maria, you really worked hard in group, and I'm glad
> you helped me like me a lot better."

Group members drop their "warm fuzzy" statements in the appropriate person's bag. If the children agree, they can share some of
these positive statements with the group.

Thank-You Cards

This activity can be done with almost all ages. You will need colored
construction paper and crayons or marking pens for everyone.

Each child takes a piece of construction paper, folds it in half so it looks like a greeting card, traces his or her hand on the front, and writes his or her name inside of the hand. (The hand is one's own very personal symbol of sharing with others.) Then each child passes his or her card to the child on the left so that child can write a line inside. The cards circulate until everyone has written something on everyone else's card.

Group Poem

> This activity is magical! Group members, especially those of middle school age, love it and think it is very special.

Give each child a piece of paper and a marking pen. Have the children write their initials in the top right-hand corner of the paper (do this on your own sheet of paper as well). Each child writes a short line to start a poem at the top of his or her paper. Each child then passes the paper to the person on the left, and that person looks at the line and adds another line to the poem. When everyone has added a line, the poem is returned to the original owner.

You may need to give an example if group members don't know what you mean when you tell them to "write a line." Some examples of starting lines are:

We've learned a lot and grown a lot . . .

Our group is like a flower that blooms . . .

I feel so good, I know much more . . .

My family has changed and so have I . . .

Friendships are special—I'm special too . . .

I'm not afraid to be angry any more . . .

After the poems are complete, first share your own, then ask the rest of the group members whether they are willing to share theirs. If the group agrees, you can collect all of the poems and make a copy of each child's poem for each other child in the group.

Party!

Even the youngest group members enjoy sharing food at the last session. You can get funds for a pizza and soda or cake and ice cream from various sources—if your group is held in a school, you could request help from your guidance committee, composed of parents, teachers, and community members. If the group members are older, they may be willing to "pitch in" by bringing different food items. I like to order a cake with "congratulations" and all the group members' names written in icing. Group members love having the piece with their name on it, and it is a special treat for working on their behaviors and learning new skills.

ETHICAL GUIDELINES FOR GROUP COUNSELORS

Preamble

One characteristic of any professional group is the possession of a body of knowledge, skills, and voluntarily self-professed standards for ethical practice. A Code of Ethics consists of those standards that have been formally and publicly acknowledged by the members of a profession to serve as the guidelines for professional conduct, discharge of duties, and the resolution of moral dilemmas. By this document, the Association for Specialists in Group Work (ASGW) has identified the standards of conduct appropriate for ethical behavior among its members. The Association for Specialists in Group Work recognizes the basic commitment of its members to the Ethical Standards of its parent organization, the American Association for Counseling and Development (AACD) and nothing in this document shall be construed to supplant that code. These standards are intended to complement the AACD standards in the area of group work by clarifying the nature of ethical responsibility of the counselor in the group setting and by stimulating a greater concern for competent group leadership. The group counselor is expected to be a professional agent and to take the processes of ethical responsibility seriously. ASGW views "ethical process" as being integral to group work and views group counselors as "ethical agents." Group counselors, by their very nature in being responsible and responsive to their group members, necessarily embrace a certain potential for ethical vulnerability. It is incumbent upon group counselors to give considerable attention to the intent and context of their actions because the attempts of counselors to influence human behavior through group work always have ethical implications.

The following ethical guidelines have been developed to encourage ethical behavior of group counselors. These guidelines are written for students and practitioners, and are meant to stimulate reflection, self-examination, and discussion of issues and practices. They address the group counselor's responsibility for providing information about group work to clients and the group counselor's responsibility for providing group counseling services to clients. A final section discusses the group counselor's responsibility for

Reprinted from *Journal for Specialists in Group Work*, 15(2), 1990, pp. 119–126. No further reproduction authorized without written permission of the American Counseling Association.

safeguarding ethical practice and procedures for reporting unethi-cal behavior. Group counselors are expected to make known these standards to group members.

Ethical Guidelines

1. *Orientation and providing information:* Group counselors adequately prepare prospective or new group members by providing as much information about the existing or proposed group as necessary. Minimally, information related to each of the following areas should be provided.

   (a) Entrance procedures, time parameters of the group experience, group participation expectations, methods of payment (where appropriate), and termination procedures are explained by the group counselor as appropriate to the level of maturity of group members and the nature and purpose(s) of the group.

   (b) Group counselors have available for distribution a professional disclosure statement that includes information on the group counselor's qualifications and group services that can be provided, particularly as related to the nature and purpose(s) of the specific group.

   (c) Group counselors communicate the role expectations, rights, and responsibilities of group members and group counselor(s).

   (d) The group goals are stated as concisely as possible by the group counselor, including "whose" goal it is (the group counselor's, the institution's, the parent's, the law's, society's, etc.) and the role of group members in influencing or determining the group's goal(s).

   (e) Group counselors explore with group members the risks of potential life changes that may occur because of the group experience and help members explore their readiness to face these possibilities.

   (f) Group members are informed by the group counselor of unusual or experimental procedures that might be expected in their group experience.

(g) Group counselors explain, as realistically as possible, what services can and cannot be provided within the particular group structure offered.

(h) Group counselors emphasize the need to promote full psychological functioning and presence among group members. They inquire from prospective group members whether they are using any kind of drug or medication that may affect functioning in the group. They do not permit any use of alcohol and/or illegal drugs during group sessions and they discourage the use of alcohol and/or drugs (legal or illegal) prior to group meetings which may affect the physical or emotional presence of the member or other group members.

(i) Group counselors inquire from prospective group members whether they have ever been a client in counseling or psychotherapy. If a prospective group member is already in a counseling relationship with another professional person, the group counselor advises the prospective group member to notify the other professional of his or her participation in the group.

(j) Group counselors clearly inform group members about the policies pertaining to the group counselor's willingness to consult with them between group sessions.

(k) In establishing fees for group counseling services, group counselors consider the financial status and the locality of prospective group members. Group members are not charged fees for group sessions where the group counselor is not present and the policy of charging for sessions missed by a group member is clearly communicated. Fees for participating as a group member are contracted between group counselor and group member for a specified period of time. Group counselors do not increase fees for group counseling services until the existing contracted fee structure has expired. In the event that the established fee structure is inappropriate for a prospective member, group counselors assist in finding comparable services of acceptable cost.

2. *Screening of members:* The group counselor screens prospective group members (when appropriate to their theoretical orientation). Insofar as possible, the counselor selects group members whose needs and goals are compatible with the goals of the group, who will not impede the group process, and whose well being will not be jeopardized by the group experience. An orientation to the group (i.e., ASGW Ethical Guideline #1) is included during the screening process. Screening may be accomplished in one or more ways, such as the following:

   (a) Individual interview

   (b) Group interview of prospective group members

   (c) Interview as part of a team staffing

   (d) Completion of a written questionnaire by prospective group members

3. *Confidentiality:* Group counselors protect members by defining clearly what confidentiality means, why it is important, and the difficulties involved in enforcement.

   (a) Group counselors take steps to protect members by defining confidentiality and the limits of confidentiality (i.e., when a group member's condition indicates that there is clear and imminent danger to the member, others, or physical property, the group counselor takes reasonable personal action and/or informs responsible authorities).

   (b) Group counselors stress the importance of confidentiality and set a norm of confidentiality regarding all group participants' disclosures. The importance of maintaining confidentiality is emphasized before the group begins and at various times in the group. The fact that confidentiality cannot be guaranteed is clearly stated.

   (c) Members are made aware of the difficulties involved in enforcing and ensuring confidentiality in a group setting. The counselor provides examples of how confidentiality can nonmaliciously be broken to increase members' awareness, and helps to lessen the likelihood that this breach of confidence will occur. Group counselors inform group members about the potential consequences of intentionally breaching confidentiality.

(d) Group counselors can only ensure confidentiality on their part and not on the part of the members.

(e) Group counselors videotape or audiotape a group session only with the prior consent and the members' knowledge of how the tape will be used.

(f) When working with minors, the group counselor specifies the limits of confidentiality.

(g) Participants in a mandatory group are made aware of any reporting procedures required of the group counselor.

(h) Group counselors store or dispose of group member records (written, audio, video, etc.) in ways that maintain confidentiality.

(i) Instructors of group counseling courses maintain the anonymity of group members whenever discussing group counseling cases.

4. *Voluntary/involuntary participation:* Group counselors inform members whether participation is voluntary or involuntary.

(a) Group counselors take steps to ensure informed consent procedures in both voluntary and involuntary groups.

(b) When working with minors in a group, counselors are expected to follow the procedures specified by the institution in which they are practicing.

(c) With involuntary groups, every attempt is made to enlist the cooperation of the members and their continuance in the group on a voluntary basis.

(d) Group counselors do not certify that group treatment has been received by members who merely attend sessions but did not meet the defined group expectations. Group members are informed about the consequences for failing to participate in a group.

5. *Leaving a group:* Provisions are made to assist a group member to terminate in an effective way.

(a) Procedures to be followed for a group member who chooses to exit a group prematurely are discussed by the counselor with all group members either before the group begins, during a prescreening interview, or during the initial group session.

(b) In case of legally mandated group counseling, group counselors inform members of the possible consequences for premature self-termination.

(c) Ideally, both the group counselor and the member can work cooperatively to determine the degree to which a group experience is productive or counterproductive for that individual.

(d) Members ultimately have a right to discontinue membership in the group, at a designated time, if the predetermined trial period proves to be unsatisfactory.

(e) Members have the right to exit a group, but it is important that they be made aware of the importance of informing the counselor and the group members prior to deciding to leave. The counselor discusses the possible risks of leaving the group prematurely with a member who is considering this option.

(f) Before leaving a group, the group counselor encourages members (if appropriate) to discuss their reasons for wanting to discontinue membership in the group. Counselors intervene if other members use undue pressure to force a member to remain in the group.

6. *Coercion and pressure:* Group counselors protect member rights against physical threats, intimidation, coercion, and undue peer pressure insofar as is reasonably possible.

(a) It is essential to differentiate between "therapeutic pressure" that is part of any group and "undue pressure," which is not therapeutic.

(b) The purpose of a group is to help participants find their own answers, not to pressure them into doing what the group thinks is appropriate.

(c) Counselors exert care not to coerce participants to change in directions which they clearly state they do not choose.

(d) Counselors have responsibility to intervene when others use undue pressure or attempt to persuade members against their will.

(e) Counselors intervene when any member attempts to act out aggression in a physical way that might harm another member or themselves.

(f) Counselors intervene when a member is verbally abusive or inappropriately confrontive to another member.

7. *Imposing counselor values:* Group counselors develop an awareness of their own values and needs and the potential impact they have on the interventions likely to be made.

(a) Although group counselors take care to avoid imposing their values on members, it is appropriate that they expose their own beliefs, decisions, needs, and values when concealing them would create problems for the members.

(b) There are values implicit in any group, and these are made clear to potential members before they join the group. (Examples of certain values include: expressing feelings, being direct and honest, sharing personal material with others, learning how to trust, improving interpersonal communication, and deciding for oneself.)

(c) Personal and professional needs of group counselors are not met at the members' expense.

(d) Group counselors avoid using the group for their own therapy.

(e) Group counselors are aware of their own values and assumptions and how these apply in a multicultural context.

(f) Group counselors take steps to increase their awareness of ways that their personal reactions to members might inhibit the group process and they monitor their countertransference. Through an awareness of the impact of stereotyping and discrimination (i.e., biases based on age, disability, ethnicity, gender, race, religion, or sexual preference), group counselors guard the individual rights and personal dignity of all group members.

8. *Equitable treatment:* Group counselors make every reasonable effort to treat each member individually and equally.

   (a) Group counselors recognize and respect differences (e.g., cultural, racial, religious, life style, age, disability, gender) among group members.

   (b) Group counselors maintain an awareness of their behavior toward individual group members and are alert to the potential detrimental effects of favoritism or partiality toward any particular group member to the exclusion or detriment of any other member(s). It is likely that group counselors will favor some members over others, yet all group members deserve to be treated equally.

   (c) Group counselors ensure equitable use of group time for each member by inviting silent members to become involved, acknowledging nonverbal attempts to communicate, and discouraging rambling and monopolizing of time by members.

   (d) If a large group is planned, counselors consider enlisting another qualified professional to serve as a co-leader for the group sessions.

9. *Dual relationships:* Group counselors avoid dual relationships with group members that might impair their objectivity and professional judgment, as well as those which are likely to compromise a group member's ability to participate fully in the group.

   (a) Group counselors do not misuse their professional role and power as group leader to advance personal or social contacts with members throughout the duration of the group.

   (b) Group counselors do not use their professional relationship with group members to further their own interest either during the group or after the termination of the group.

   (c) Sexual intimacies between group counselors and members are unethical.

   (d) Group counselors do not barter (exchange) professional services with group members for services.

(e) Group counselors do not admit their own family members, relatives, employees, or personal friends as members to their groups.

(f) Group counselors discuss with group members the potential detrimental effects of group members' engaging in intimate intermember relationships outside of the group.

(g) Students who participate in a group as a partial course requirement for a group course are not evaluated for an academic grade based upon their degree of participation as a member in a group. Instructors of group counseling courses take steps to minimize the possible negative impact on students when they participate in a group course by separating course grades from participation in the group and by allowing students to decide what issues to explore and when to stop.

(h) It is inappropriate to solicit members from a class (or institutional affiliation) for one's private counseling or therapeutic groups.

10. *Use of techniques:* Group counselors do not attempt any technique unless trained in its use or under supervision by a counselor familiar with the intervention.

(a) Group counselors are able to articulate a theoretical orientation that guides their practice, and they are able to provide a rationale for their interventions.

(b) Depending upon the type of intervention, group counselors have training commensurate with the potential impact of a technique.

(c) Group counselors are aware of the necessity to modify their techniques to fit the unique needs of various cultural and ethnic groups.

(d) Group counselors assist members in translating in-group learnings to daily life.

11. *Goal development:* Group counselors make every effort to assist members in developing their personal goals.

(a) Group counselors use their skills to assist members in making their goals specific so that others present in the group will understand the nature of the goals.

(b) Throughout the course of a group, group counselors assist members in assessing the degree to which personal goals are being met and assist in revising any goals when it is appropriate.

(c) Group counselors help members clarify the degree to which the goals can be met within the context of a particular group.

12. *Consultation:* Group counselors develop and explain policies about between-session consultation to group members.

(a) Group counselors take care to make certain that members do not use between-session consultations to avoid dealing with issues pertaining to the group that would be dealt with best in the group.

(b) Group counselors urge members to bring the issues discussed during between-session consultations into the group if they pertain to the group.

(c) Group counselors seek out consultation and/or supervision regarding ethical concerns or when encountering difficulties which interfere with their effective functioning as group leaders.

(d) Group counselors seek appropriate professional assistance for their own personal problems or conflicts that are likely to impair their professional judgment and work performance.

(e) Group counselors discuss their group cases only for professional consultation and educational purposes.

(f) Group counselors inform members about policies regarding whether consultations will be held confidential.

13. *Termination from the group:* Depending upon the purpose of participation in the group, counselors promote termination of members from the group in the most efficient period of time.

(a) Group counselors maintain a constant awareness of the progress made by each group member and periodically invite the group members to explore and reevaluate their experiences in the group. It is the responsibility of group counselors to help promote the independence of members from the group in a timely manner.

14. *Evaluation and follow up:* Group counselors make every attempt to engage in ongoing assessment and to design follow-up procedures for their groups.

   (a) Group counselors recognize the importance of ongoing assessment of a group, and they assist members in evaluating their own progress.

   (b) Group counselors conduct evaluation of the total group experience at the final meeting (or before termination), as well as ongoing evaluation.

   (c) Group counselors monitor their own behavior and become aware of what they are modeling in the group.

   (d) Follow-up procedures might take the form of personal contact, telephone contact, or written contact.

   (e) Follow-up meetings might be with individuals, groups, or both to determine the degree to which: (i) members have reached their goals, (ii) the group had a positive or negative effect on the participants, and (iii) members could profit from some type of referral. Information is requested for possible modification of future groups. If there is no follow-up meeting, provisions are made available for individual follow-up meetings to any member who needs or requests such a contact.

15. *Referrals:* If the needs of a particular member cannot be met within the type of group being offered, the group counselor suggests other appropriate professional referrals.

   (a) Group counselors are knowledgeable of local community resources for assisting group members regarding professional referrals.

   (b) Group counselors help members seek further professional assistance, if needed.

16. *Professional development:* Group counselors recognize that professional growth is a continuous, ongoing, developmental process throughout their career.

(a) Group counselors maintain and upgrade their knowledge and skill competencies through educational activities, clinical experiences, and participation in professional development activities.

(b) Group counselors keep abreast of research findings and new developments as applied to groups.

Safeguarding Ethical Practice and Procedures for Reporting Unethical Behavior

The preceding remarks have been advanced as guidelines which are generally representative of ethical and professional group practice. They have not been proposed as rigidly defined prescriptions. However, practitioners who are thought to be grossly unresponsive to the ethical concerns addressed in this document may be subject to a review of their practices by the AACD Ethics Committee and ASGW peers. For consultation and/or questions regarding these ASGW Ethical Guidelines or group ethical dilemmas, you may contact the Chairperson of the ASGW Ethics Committee. The name, address, and telephone number of the current ASGW Ethics Committee Chairperson may be acquired by telephoning the AACD office in Alexandria, Virginia at (703) 823–9800.

If a group counselor's behavior is suspected as being unethical, the following procedures are to be followed:

(a) Collect more information and investigate further to confirm the unethical practice as determined by the ASGW Ethical Guidelines.

(b) Confront the individual with the apparent violation of ethical guidelines for the purposes of protecting the safety of any clients and to help the group counselor correct any inappropriate behaviors. If satisfactory resolution is not reached through this contact then:

(c) A complaint should be made in writing, including the specific facts and dates of the alleged violation and all relevant supporting data. The complaint should be included in an envelope marked "CONFIDENTIAL" to ensure confidentiality for both the accuser(s) and the alleged violator(s) and forwarded to all of the following sources:

1. The name and address of the Chairperson of the state Counselor Licensure Board for the respective state, if in existence.

2. The Ethics Committee, c/o The President, American Association for Counseling and Development, 5999 Stevenson Avenue, Alexandria, VA 22304.

3. The name and address of all private credentialing agencies in which the alleged violator maintains credentials or holds professional membership. Some of these include the following:

National Board for Certified Counselors, Inc.
3D Terrace Way
Greensboro, NC 27403

National Council for Credentialing of Career Counselors
c/o NBCC
5999 Stevenson Avenue
Alexandria, VA 22304

National Academy for Certified Clinical Mental Health
  Counselors
5999 Stevenson Avenue
Alexandria, VA 22304

Commission on Rehabilitation Counselor Certification
162 North State Street
Suite 317
Chicago, IL 60601

American Association for Marriage and Family Therapy
1717 K Street, N. W., Suite 407
Washington, DC 20006

American Psychological Association
1200 Seventeenth Street, N. W.
Washington, DC 20036

American Group Psychotherapy Association, Inc.
25 East 21st Street, 6th Floor
New York, New York 10010

TAP-IN SELECTION CHECKLIST

Date _____ Interviewer _____

Name of client _____

Age _____ Group topic _____

Tell

_____ 1. The topic the group will address (e.g., divorce, grief, anger management), purpose of the group, and what you hope to accomplish as leader.

_____ 2. Where, when, and how often the group is scheduled to meet.

_____ 3. If and how any missed academic work may be made up.

_____ 4. Who will be leading the group.

_____ 5. The nature of group members (e.g., other fifth and sixth graders, other youths from the hospital or community with the same problems).

_____ 6. To be in the group, you must give your written permission, and your parents or guardian must also sign a statement that you may be in the group.

_____ 7. Being a group member will require you to share some of your personal thoughts, feelings, and behaviors, but only those you choose to share. No one will force you to talk about things you consider private and don't want to share.

_____ 8. As the group leader, I have the responsibility to protect group members from being harmed physically or verbally by other group members. For everyone's safety, no one is allowed to hit or fight or hurt other group members.

_____ 9. You have the responsibility to attend all sessions unless you talk to me ahead of time and arrange not to be there or to leave the group.

_____ 10. *(For involuntary members only)* If you choose to stop coming to group, [the court or other entity] has determined that the consequences are [state the specific consequences].

_____ 11. You have the right to leave the group at any time, provided you discuss this with me and come to one final session to tell the group good-bye. In the group each member becomes very important to each other member, and saying good-bye is necessary.

_____ 12. You have the responsibility to make an effort to understand your problems and to set goals to make positive changes. You also have the right to change these goals.

_____ 13. *(If the member is required to change behaviors—e.g., by the court)* You will be required to work toward changing [name the specific behaviors]. If you do not work on these behaviors, I will [describe the specific consequences].

_____ 14. In group everyone agrees to keep whatever is said in group confidential. This means that no one tells what anyone else says or does in group. The other group members will agree not to tell what you say or do in group, and you must agree not to tell what they say or do in group. Because we don't ever have control over what someone else says or does, we can't be sure everyone will keep this promise. At the beginning of each session I will remind everyone about the confidentiality rule, and this will help us remember.

What would you like to ask me about this?

_____ 15. There are some times when I would need to share what you say with other adults, such as your parents or guardian. These times are:

If you say you are going to harm yourself or someone else.

If you say anything about child abuse happening to yourself or someone else.

If the court (a judge) tells me I need to share the information.

What would you like to ask me about this?

_____ 16. *(For involuntary group members only)* If you are coming to a group because a judge or your probation officer requires it, you need to know that I must report back about whether or not you are making an effort to change, just coming to group but not participating, or not coming to group on a regular basis.

_____ 17. I have a policy about meeting with group members between sessions. If you have a problem with something that involves confidentiality or a serious problem about something that is not related to what is going on in the group, then I could meet with you between sessions. But if you want to talk about things that could best be dealt with among group members, then I may not talk with you between sessions.

_____ 18. Being in group can be good for you because you have a support system to help you and new ideas from others your age, you meet others who are struggling with the same problems, and you can practice new behaviors in a safe place.

_____ 19. Being in group also has certain risks. Other group members might try to pressure you to change when you are not ready or to try behaviors you are unsure about. It is part of my job to try to keep other members from pressuring you against your choice.

_____ 20. Another risk of being in the group is that I cannot guarantee that other group members will keep what you say confidential; someone might repeat something you said outside of the group.

_____ 21. Sometimes other people in your life are not ready or willing for you to make changes, and they might question or pressure you if you change. This can be uncomfortable. The other members and I will help you with this, but you need to know that this is a possible risk of being in the group.

_____ 22. I will make sure that all group members get an equal chance to talk.

_____ 23. You will be expected to come on time for each meeting. We will work out the schedule with you, your teachers, and your parents or guardian to make sure that you are free at the time of the group sessions. Once the group starts, the members share things and the group gets to be very important. If one member doesn't come on time, it affects everyone.

_____ 24. In group we sometimes practice new ways of doing things. You will be expected to practice new skills in group and sometimes outside of group between sessions. Practice between sessions is sometimes called "self-improvement homework."

Ask

_____ 1. What questions do you have about what I've said so far?

_____ 2. What else would you like to know about group? About the leader(s)?

_____ 3. Are you going to any other counselors or psychologists for counseling in a group or by yourself?

_____ 4. If you are chosen for the group, will you come to each meeting and come on time?

_____ 5. Are you willing to share your ideas and feelings and behaviors with the group?

_____ 6. Are you willing to do self-improvement homework between sessions?

_____ 7. Are you willing to keep what the other members say in group confidential?

_____ 8. Do you understand that there are some special times I might need to share what you say in group with other adults, such as your parents or guardian?

_____ 9. What would you most like to learn about in group?

_____ 10. What behaviors would you like to change?

_____ 11. What goal would you most like to accomplish?

_____ 12. *(Only if applicable)* Would you give your permission to audiotape or videotape the group session if you could ask to have the tape turned off if you felt uncomfortable?

_____ 13. On a scale of 1 to 10, with 1 meaning very little and 10 meaning a whole lot, how much do you want to be in the group?

Note: This completes the interview portion with the child. Complete the "pick" portion after the interview with the child is finished.

Pick

_____ 1. Does the child seem to understand what the purpose and goals of the group are?

_____ 2. Does the child appear to want to participate in and be a productive member of the group?

_____ 3. Does the child have some positive behaviors/attitudes that would serve as a model for some of the other potential members?

_____ 4. Does the child seem compatible with the other group members tentatively selected?

_____ 5. Does the child appear to be making the decision to join the group independently or under the influence of others?

_____ 6. Does the child appear to be giving assent?

_____ 7. What is the child's motivation factor (on a scale of 1 to 10)?

Selected _____ Not selected _____

Potential for future group? Yes _____ No _____

Comments _____

_____

_____

_____

ABOUT THE AUTHOR

Rosemarie Smead is Professor and Coordinator of Counselor Education at Indiana University Southeast in New Albany. Dr. Smead is an accomplished teacher and training consultant, with over 20 years experience working with children and adolescents in school, mental health, inpatient, and family therapy settings. She has presented workshops and training seminars both nationally and internationally to various professional groups, state departments of education, school systems, juvenile treatment facilities, and business and industry. Dr. Smead is past president and fellow of the Association for Specialists in Group Work and has received state, ASGW, and university awards for her distinguished teaching and service to the profession in group work. She holds a doctorate in counseling psychology from Auburn University, is a licensed marriage and family therapist, and is a clinical member of the American Association for Marriage and Family Therapists. In addition to her program coordination and teaching responsibilities, she consults with and conducts workshops for school systems, mental health agencies, government agencies, professional organizations, and hospital treatment facilities. Her professional interests are in counselor education and group counseling research with children and adolescents, and she maintains a private practice in marriage and family therapy. She is the author of the widely acclaimed books *Skills for Living: Group Counseling Activities for Young Adolescents* (Research Press, 1990) and *Skills for Living: Group Counseling Activities for Elementary Students* (Research Press, 1994), both written under the name Rosemarie Smead Morganett.